52 Fun Family Devotions

Mike & Amy Nappa

Augsburg
MINNEAPOLIS

For Tony,
who makes it fun to be a family.

52 FUN FAMILY DEVOTIONS
Exploring and Discovering God's Word

Copyright © 1994 Augsburg Fortress. All rights reserved. Except for brief quotations in critical articles or reviews, no part of this book may be reproduced in any manner without prior written permission from the publisher. Write to: Permissions, Augsburg Fortress, 426 S. Fifth St., Box 1209, Minneapolis, MN 55440.

Scriptures quoted from *Youth Bible*, New Century Version, copyright © 1991 by Word Publishing, Dallas, Texas 75234. All rights reserved.

Cover design and interior illustrations: Cindy Cobb Olson
Interior design: Judy Gilats, Peregrine Graphics Services

Library of Congress Cataloging-in-Publication Data

Nappa, Mike, 1963–
    52 fun family devotions : exploring and discovering God's word /
by Mike and Amy Nappa.
        p.   cm.
    Includes index.
    ISBN 0-8066-2698-4 (alk. paper) :
    1. Family—Prayer—books and devotions—English.   2. Devotional
calendars.   3. Spiritual life—Christianity.   I. Nappa, Amy, 1963–
. II. Title.
BV255.N37   1994
249—dc20   93-47945
                                                                    CIP

The paper used in this publication meets the minimum requirements of American National Standard for Information Sciences—Permanence of Paper for Printed Library Materials, ANSI Z329.48-1984.   (∞)™

Manufactured in the U.S.A.   AF 9-2698

98   97   96   95   94   1   2   3   4   5   6   7   8   9   10

Contents

Introduction

A Creative God Deserves Creative Learning

It was probably when he first stood up in the belly of the whale that Jonah thought to himself, "I'll bet God is trying to teach me something . . ."

Now, that was an innovative object lesson! When God had a message for this fleeing prophet, no time was wasted by sending a certified letter. Instead God sent a great fish to communicate personally the importance of God's words. The rest is history.

The prophet Jonah is not the only person with whom God went to great lengths to communicate. The Bible is full of exciting examples of God working creatively in order to become known to His children. Just take a look at this sampling of God's handiwork:

- When God wanted to catch Moses' attention, God set a bush on fire but did not let it burn (Exodus 3:1-6).
- In order to correct an erring prophet, God made a donkey talk (Numbers 22:21-35).
- To illustrate new life to Ezekiel, God turned a valley of dry bones into a multitude of people (Ezekiel 37:1-14).
- By delivering Daniel from the den of lions, God showed King Nebuchadnezzar the value of prayer (Daniel 6:1-23).
- When God wanted to express his love for all people, he sent his Son to die for our sins (John 3:16).

Same Old Script

With this rich history of creative communication, you would think that we would have no problems sharing the Word of God with our family members. Yet the struggle to maintain an interesting and relevant family devotion time is one we all face. Sometimes it seems all devotions follow the same script:

"Who will read this week's Scripture?" a parent asks the family members gathered around the dining room table.

Silence.

"Okay, I'll go ahead and read it," the parent continues. After the reading of Psalm 23, it's time for discussion. "So, what do you think of this passage?"

More silence.

Finally one parent ventures an answer in the hope it will spark conversation. "I think it's a wonderful verse about how God watches over us. What do you think, Billy?"

Billy is caught off guard. He was daydreaming about Shaquille O'Neal and the Orlando Magic. "Uh, I agree with you one hundred percent."

"Me too!" pipes up five-year-old Rachael.

Diane finally enters the conversation. "Wow! I have never learned so much about God in my life! May I be excused now? My date will be here in less than three hours and I still have to do my hair."

"Well, okay," answers the parent. "Unless anyone else has any more thoughts on this verse?"

No response.

"Then I guess we should close in prayer."

Thirty seconds after the "Amen," the parent stares at an empty table and wonders why no one seems to get much out of family devotions.

Experiential Learning

Most Christian parents would agree that group devotions are an important part of family life. Unfortunately, many parents have also found that their kids would rather take out the trash than sit through another boring half hour of household time with God.

Perhaps it's time for families to catch on to what educators have known for years: people learn by doing. If you read a Scripture and talk about being fishers of men to your children, they will remember only 5 to 10 percent of what you tell them. If you take your family on a fishing trip and discuss how that activity relates to fishing for souls, your kids will remember 80 to 90 percent of your lesson. Why? Because they have experienced it, not just heard about it.

That's the basis of experiential learning. It's a process involving the five senses, not only one or two. It makes learning a thing to be lived—seen, heard, breathed, tasted, and touched. It can literally make the Bible come alive for your children.

No More Bible Study Blahs!

52 Fun Family Devotions is designed to help parents do just that. Based on the concept of experiential learning, it's chock-full of creative ideas parents can use to communicate biblical principles to children of all ages. It provides a way for families to breathe new life into their weekly devotions. No more Bible study blahs!

With minimal preparation a parent can use this book to lead the family in a time of exploration and discovery from God's Word. First, everyone participates in a fun activity, called Exploration. Then, using questions based on the activity, the parent leads a discussion to encourage the Discovery of the priceless treasures of Scriptures.

There are scores of creative ideas for family devotions in this book. Take a moment to browse through the pages and see what activities would appeal to your family. Then try them out. You'll find they are a lot like potato chips. You can't stop with just one!

These Devotions Are Different!

This book is unlike other guides to family devotions. Instead of sitting around the table and listening to one person read the Bible, you'll be involving your family in a wide range of experiences. These may take place in your home or at a variety of locations. You might need to gather a few supplies or make special arrangements beforehand. These tips will help you prepare for your devotional adventures:

■ Plan a weekly time to have devotions and stick to it. Mark this time on the calendar and ask each person to plan his or her activities accordingly. No one will want to miss out!

■ Designate one person to prepare for the coming week's devotion. This person can be an adult or older child. If your family is large enough, let various members take turns planning the devotion. Learning about God isn't just something adults teach kids. We all have something to offer.

■ The person leading the devotion will need to read the entire devotion ahead of time. Doing this the day before your family meets together will allow time to gather various supplies or make arrangements as specified in the devotions.

■ It may be necessary to adjust devotions according to your family size and structure. A single parent with one child may want to modify devotions calling for two teams. If your child is old enough, each of you may become a team of one. Or you can join together and complete the activity without competition.

■ Perhaps you're raising your grandkids or merely have them over for occasional overnight visits. These devotions will work for you too. Whether your family group includes cousins, foster family members, or even neighbor kids over for a visit, everyone can participate and learn!

Helpful Hints for Developing Your Own Family Devotions

Fun family devotions don't have to end with the last page of this book. You can create more activities tailored to your family's needs and interests. Here are a few tips:

■ Look for activities your family already enjoys and use these to teach biblical truths. For example, during a "seventh inning stretch" at a baseball game, talk about the importance of working together as a sports team. Relate this to working together on "God's team," the church.

■ Identify areas in which your family struggles, and look for creative ways to understand God's perspective on these issues. Perhaps your kids pick at each other, constantly putting each other down. Try placing an unfrosted cake on your dinner table and pick it apart during the meal, leaving a large pile of crumbs. (Just smile when your family questions your behavior!)

After dinner, ask someone to read Galatians 5:15 and relate how words can destroy people like picking at a cake destroys dessert. Then sprinkle the crumbs over ice cream and spend some time building each other up while enjoying a treat.

■ Make planning a family affair. Have older kids help organize activities. Or have an older and younger child work together in leading a devotion, letting them teach *you* a lesson! If your family includes a wide spread of ages, work in teams so everyone is involved.

■ Look for teachable moments. The idea here is not to be overly spiritual, but to recognize that God is a part of every aspect of our lives. While feeding the ducks with your preschooler, for example, comment on how God wants us to care for animals. Then ask her to think of ways God cares for her and how she can care for others.

■ Have fun! Keep the tone light without getting too competitive in the activities. Make sure everyone wins at games. Get in there with your kids and enjoy the time together as a participant. This is *family* fun!

1.

Microwave Popsicles

Focus: Peer pressure

Scripture Reference: Romans 12:1-2

In the first century A.D., Rome existed as the center of a Roman world characterized by immorality and decadence. It was also home to many first-century Christians. As these Christians lived daily in a thoroughly non-Christian society, Paul warned them in Romans 12:1-2 to become like God, not like the people of the world.

Families today live in a society not unlike ancient Rome. Family members of all ages are pressured to conform to the world's standards. "Cheat to get ahead." "Look out for number one." "Everybody's having sex—just use a condom." "Popularity equals power." Use this devotion to show your family how Paul's warning to the ancient Romans is still relevant today.

Equipment: Popsicles, microwave oven, bowls, and a Bible

Exploration: Tell the family that you are going to have the latest trendy dessert that *everyone* is eating these days. Pull some popsicles out of the freezer and place them, wrappers and all, in the microwave. Cook them until they are good and soggy, and then hand them out to family members (bowls and napkins may be needed). Be sure no one gets burned by a hot wrapper or popsicle juice.

Now point out the obvious: Microwaving popsicles may be trendy, but it's also a pretty stupid way to eat a frozen treat. Popsicles are not meant to be cooked.

Share with your family how people are often encouraged by their friends, commercials, advertisements, celebrities, and society to do things that aren't very smart. This is often like trying to eat microwaved popsicles. It's not what the maker intended.

Discovery: Read Romans 12:1-2 and discuss these questions:

- How did you feel when I handed you the microwaved popsicles?
- How is microwaving popsicles like following some of the trends our friends follow?
- What are some of the ways the world tries to get us and our friends to do everything it does? What can we do when these actions or ideas are not smart or are against God's plans?
- What are the rewards of following God instead of the world?

Prayer: Lead your family in a short prayer like this: "Lord, give us wisdom to be able to recognize when others encourage us to follow them instead of you. Give us the strength to follow the encouragement of Romans 12:1-2 this week and for the rest of our lives. In Jesus' name, amen."

Then pass out frozen popsicles for everyone to enjoy.

2.

Thankfulness Murals

Focus: Thankfulness

Scripture Reference: Luke 17:11-19

Luke 17:11-19 tells the story of Jesus healing the ten lepers. Nine who were healed went on with their lives. One came back to Jesus simply to say "thanks."

When was the last time your family paused to say "thanks" to God? Last Thanksgiving? New Year's Day?

Use this devotion to encourage your family to make thankfulness a part of everyday life.

Equipment: Butcher paper (or white shelf paper), colored markers, and a Bible

Exploration: Spread the paper over the dining room or kitchen table. Have each family member take a seat around the table. (If your table isn't large enough for this activity, use the floor.) Pass out markers to everyone and instruct them to make a mural full of pictures of things for which they are thankful.

When everyone is finished, take turns sharing your pictures with the whole family. Then remove the paper from the table and hang it in the kitchen, hallway, or another common area as a reminder of what they have been given.

Discovery: Discuss the following questions:
■ Was it difficult or easy to think of things to draw? Why?
■ Why did you choose to draw the things you did? What other things could you add to the mural?
■ How do you show your thankfulness to God? To others?
  Read Luke 17:11-19 and talk about these questions:
■ Why do you think only one leper came back to thank Jesus?
■ How would you have felt if you had been Jesus? How do you think Jesus actually felt?
■ Who in the story are you most like? What can we do to help ourselves become better at expressing our gratitude to God and others?

Prayer: Sit in a circle and ask everyone to hold hands. Have family members take turns telling one specific reason they're thankful for each person in the circle. Then close with a prayer of thanks for the way each family member contributes to your family as a whole.

3

The Memory Game

Focus: Forgiveness

Scripture References: Jeremiah 31:34b, Psalm 103:12

The last half of Jeremiah 31:34 and all of Psalm 103:12 give beautiful promises of God's forgiveness. How many of a Christian's sins will God remember? None. How far has God taken our sins away? As far as the east is from the west—farther than we can imagine or explore. These promises of forgiveness hold no age limit. From the youngest child to the oldest grandparent, all can benefit from God's loving mercy. Use this devotion to remind your family members of God's "bad memory" when it comes to sin.

Equipment: A deck of cards and a Bible

Exploration: Shuffle a deck of cards and lay them all out individually, face down, on the table or floor. Have all participants take turns turning over any two cards. If the cards match (two queens, two eights, and so on), then the person can pick them up and take another turn. If the cards do not match, the person turns them face down again and the next person takes a turn. At the end of the game the person with the most cards wins. (If your children are very young, play this in teams pairing older family members with younger ones.)

Discovery: After the game, ask, "Would you be surprised if I told you that God has a bad memory?" Read Jeremiah 31:34b and Psalms 103:12. Ask:

■ What do these verses tell us about God's memories of our forgiven sins?

■ How can this game remind us that God forgets our sins?

■ Whose sins does God choose to forget? Why?

- How does it feel to know that God holds no grudges against us?
- If God forgives and forgets our wrongs, how should we react when others wrong us? Why?
- What are some things we need to forgive and forget in our family? How can we help each other do that?

Prayer: Form a circle and have everyone hold hands. As your closing prayer, lead your family in singing a verse or two from the hymn "Amazing Grace." End the devotion with a big family hug.

4.

Household Gladiators

Focus: Faith—Following God

Scripture Reference: John 16:33

Enemies. Natural disasters. Harsh living conditions. Poverty. Sickness. Human cruelty. These and other obstacles were ones that early American pioneers struggled to overcome in their quest to settle in the New World.

Although your family members don't have to conquer new territory, they still may struggle in their day-to-day Christian walk. Friends distract them; fighting the world's values tires them; and failure shouts at them like a heckler from the crowd. Yet they don't have to walk alone because Jesus, who defeated this world and its obstacles, walks alongside—helping them through each moment of every day. Use this devotion to help your family members take heart, because Jesus has overcome the world.

Equipment: Living room furniture, a blindfold, a big bowl of popcorn, and a Bible

Exploration: While family members are in another room in the house, rearrange the living room furniture into a big obstacle course of couches, chairs, and tables. (Be sure to put any breakable or dangerous items off to the side.)

Next, one by one, blindfold each family member and tell them you are going to lead them through the obstacle course to their popcorn reward. The only catch is that you will be guiding them only by voice from across the room. (No touching allowed!) Next, set them on their way.

After the first person's turn, it may be fun to remove his or her blindfold and together rearrange the furniture again. See who follows instructions most easily, and who has the most difficult time.

Discovery: After everyone has braved the course, serve the popcorn, read John 16:33, and discuss these questions:

■ How did you feel when you went through the obstacle course? What was the hardest part of the obstacle course? Why?

■ What are some obstacles you've experienced as one of God's followers (what makes it hard for you to follow God)?

■ How is this obstacle course like going through each day as one of God's followers?

■ How do you think Jesus' disciples felt when they encountered obstacles to serving God? Why do you think Jesus spoke these words from John 16:33 to them just before he was crucified?

■ What do you do when you face a tough situation? How can John 16:33 encourage you in those situations?

Prayer: Clear a path down the center of the obstacle course. Have everyone hold hands and walk slowly down the path. As you walk, pray a prayer like this: "Lord, it's encouraging to know that you care about our journey through this life. As we face the many obstacles that are a part of living, help us to keep our sights focused on you so that we may walk safely through to the end. In Jesus' name, amen."

5.

The Great American Ice Cream Hunt

Focus: Treasures in heaven

Scripture Reference: Matthew 6:19-21

Just say the word "treasure" and everyone's eyes light up. Visions of sunken ships laden with gold and jewels dance in our heads. The thought of hidden riches waiting to be found almost makes our mouths water.

But there is a treasure that lasts long beyond the day that gold and riches pass away—the treasure of a life lived in service to Jesus Christ. In Matthew 6:19-21 Jesus tells all who'll listen, "Don't store up treasures for yourselves here on earth . . . but . . . in heaven." Use this devotion to help your family discover the hidden treasure of Jesus' words.

Equipment: A half-gallon of solidly frozen ice cream, spoons, and a Bible

Exploration: Hide the half-gallon of ice cream somewhere in the house or yard. Have the rest of your family find this treasure before it melts. The only clues you can give are "warmer" when they are close, and "colder" when they move away from the hiding place. When the treasure is found, hand out spoons and enjoy a treat straight from the carton.

Discovery: While everyone is eating, read Matthew 6:19-21 and ask:

■ How did you feel when you were looking for the ice cream treasure? How is this like looking for treasures from God?

■ What are other treasures people work hard to get here

on earth? Will these last forever, or will they break, get stolen, or even melt like the ice cream?
- What are treasures that we can store in heaven?
- What distracts us from searching for God's treasures? How can we help each other to fight these distractions?
- In what ways is a life in service to Jesus a treasure in heaven and here on earth?

Prayer: Tell everyone that one of the treasures found in a life in service to Jesus is the ability to communicate with God. Then help your family discover the hidden treasure of listening instead of speaking in prayer. Encourage everyone to prayerfully sit and listen as they wait for God to bring home the message of this devotion in each of their hearts.

6.

Starry, Starry Night

Focus: Attributes of God—God is Creator

Scripture References: Genesis 1:14-19, Psalm 19:1

Like an artist painting a canvas, God painted the heavens with millions of brilliant lights. The sun, moon, and stars that make up such a vast part of God's creation have not gone unnoticed. The early Hebrews looked to the skies and saw the handiwork of a magnificent creator.

Today, people look to the skies for fortunes, for scientific discoveries, and for symbols of deceiving philosophies. But the sun, moon, and stars were never meant for that. Use this devotion to help your family see the Son through the brilliance of the lights in the sky.

Equipment: A flashlight, a simple book on stars and constellations from your local library (ask the librarian for help in finding something suitable for your children's ages), and a Bible

Exploration: On a dark night, take the family outside to look at the stars. If you live in a well-lit area, driving away from the city lights will improve your viewing. Take a few blankets along and have everyone lie under the stars for a free light show.

Using a book about the stars, see if you can identify some of the major constellations. Can you determine which way is north using only the stars as a guide? How far away are the stars?

Discovery: While star-gazing, read Genesis 1:14-19 and Psalm 19:1 and discuss these questions:
- How do you feel when you look at the stars?
- How powerful does God have to be to have made the stars? God even arranged them. Can you imagine God deciding where each star should go?
- Why do you think God made stars? Do they have a purpose? What is it?
- What are other things God created? God must have a great imagination to have made so many things!
- How can we care for and preserve what God has created?
- What can we learn about God since we know God is the Creator of everything?

Prayer: Lie on your backs and silently take one last look at the stars. During that silence, have family members privately speak to God, admiring God's creation, thanking God for sharing it with us, and asking for God's help in remembering to care for it as he would want us to do.

7.

Gingerbread (or Graham Cracker) Creations

Focus: Building strong families
Scripture Reference: Matthew 7:24-27

It was an odd story for a preacher to tell, but by using the language of a carpenter Jesus brought home an important point: Living life is like constructing a house. Place it on a firm foundation and it will weather any storm. Place it on a shaky foundation and it will wash away with the sand come high tide.

As your family members build their lives, they need to know the importance of the Master Carpenter's construction story. Use this devotion to encourage your family to build its life on the foundation of Jesus and his Word.

Equipment: Square gingerbread cookies (or graham crackers), "glue" made of confectioner's sugar and water, assorted candies, paper plates, and a Bible

Exploration: Using the gingerbread cookies (or graham crackers) and sugar "glue," have each family member create a house, teepee, car, or whatever they want. Encourage them to be creative. Use the assorted candies to decorate the creations. When everyone is done, allow each family member to present and describe his or her finished product.

Discovery: Read Matthew 7:24-27 and talk about these questions:
- How is building a gingerbread creation similar to building a strong family?
- What was difficult about building something out of gingerbread? What was easy?
- Gingerbread creations are made out of cookies and candy. What are homes made out of? What is difficult about building a home?
- Why is it important for a family to have a strong "foundation"? What foundations would God like us to use for our family?
- How can each of us help to build our home on a strong foundation?

Prayer: Let family members know that one important foundation in a family is prayer. Then take a few moments to ask family members to share requests they'd like others to pray about.

The maturity of prayer requests will vary depending on children's ages. However, don't allow put-downs of any requests. If Johnny wants to pray that his teddy bear won't get sick, let him! Communicate by your example that we can take all of our concerns to God, not just the "important" ones.

After everyone has shared, take a few moments to lead your family in praying for the specific needs mentioned. Check up on the requests later to see how God has answered each prayer. Remember, God answers *all* prayers, but God's way may differ from the requested answer.

8.

Garbage Plants

Focus: Planting good in our lives

Scripture Reference: Galatians 6:7-9

In Galatians 6:7-9 the Apostle Paul draws a beautiful word picture to describe the cause-and-effect relationship of our actions on our lives. This passage provides encouragement to continue doing good. As God loves us, so we will love others.

At times, families forget the truth of Galatians 6:7-9. Instead of planting love and helpfulness, family members occasionally plant neglect, unkindness, selfishness, and hurt. Use this devotion to help your family root out unhealthy plants and become a garden overflowing with the results of God's good seeds.

Equipment: Small cups or planters, dirt, flower seeds, a piece of nonorganic trash, and a Bible

Exploration: Have family members plant flower seeds in small cups or planters. Then announce that you are going to plant a "garbage flower." Retrieve some nonorganic trash (such as a bottle cap or empty can) from the garbage and plant it as others planted their seeds.

Ask each person to describe what they think their flower will look like when it blooms. Then explain the obvious: The garbage plant will never grow into anything. It will always remain trash.

Discovery: Read Galatians 6:7-9 and talk about these questions:

■ What are some kinds of "garbage" that people plant in their lives?

■ What should you do if you discover "garbage" in your life?

■ How can you plant good in your life? In other people's lives?

■ What will be the result of planting good?

■ How do you feel when you see "garbage" growing in your life? How do you feel when you see good growing?

Prayer: Have everyone stand as you offer this prayer of blessing: "May God in his infinite wisdom teach you how to plant seeds of good in your life. In his infinite grace, may God bring those seeds to harvest. In his infinite power, may God gain praise from the growth of your good seeds. Amen."

9.

Family Forts

Focus: Faith—Trusting God for protection

Scripture Reference: Psalm 46:1-3, 7

The author of Psalm 46 fairly shouts, brimming with confidence. Let the earth shake. Let the mountains fall in the sea. Let the oceans foam and roar. God is always present to help in times of trouble.

What kind of confidence in God does your family have? Is it a timidly burning faith that flickers at the slightest breeze? Or is it a blazing faith that, like the psalmist's, burns brightly in the face of life's problems? Use this devotion to fan the flame of faith among your family members.

Equipment: Sheets, blankets, and a Bible

Exploration: Use blankets and sheets to create the biggest and best fort possible. Drape the cloths over furniture, ironing boards, counters, or anything available. See if you can make a secret passage somewhere in the fort. Be sure there is room for everyone to squeeze inside!

Discovery: While sitting together in the fort, read Psalm 46:1-3 and talk about the following questions:
■ What is a fortress?
■ When do you feel like you need a protective fort? Could we build a bigger or better fort for more protection?
■ Is there a fort, or anything else, that can always protect us?
■ How is God like a fort? Do you find it hard to have faith that God can protect you?
■ Read verse 7. This verse says that *God* is a fortress. God is like the biggest and strongest fort!
■ What is one specific thing you would like God to protect you from?

Prayer: As a family, pray that each person will have faith in God for protection. Then, if you know the words or have access to a hymnal, sing the first verse of "A Mighty Fortress Is Our God."

10.

Busted!

Focus: Visible Christian living

Scripture Reference: 1 Timothy 4:12-16

In 1 Timothy 4:12-16 Paul speaks to Timothy about his personal and public life. Paul knew that others were always watching. From Timothy's example Christians could learn more about Christ, and those who weren't believers might become Christians. Through his words, actions, and attitudes Timothy was able to show others Christ in his life.

Just as Timothy was on display to first-century people, others could be watching you and your family today. People who don't know Jesus may be looking to you for an example of how Christians live. Use this devotion to help family members evaluate how visible their Christianity is to those who are watching.

Equipment: A Bible

Exploration: Tell your family, "Let's imagine it's against the law to be a Christian. If the secret police were to invade our home at this moment, would they find enough evidence to convict us of breaking the law against Christianity?"

To answer this question, take your family on a tour of each person's bedroom. In each room look for evidence that those who live there are Christians. For example, Bibles and books on Christian topics, recordings by Christian artists, inspirational posters, or even toys related to a Bible story could be considered evidence. After looking into the bedrooms, determine which, if any, family members could be convicted of being Christians.

Then continue your search throughout the common rooms of the house. Is there enough evidence to convict your family as a whole? When your search is complete, sit down together and move on to Discovery.

Discovery: Read 1 Timothy 4:12-16 together and discuss these questions:
- How does this passage say we should be showing others what we believe?
- Let's put aside the physical evidence we looked at already. If someone were to spend a day with our family, would they know we're Christians? Why or why not?
- What keeps others from knowing or believing we're Christians? Why?
- Using the verses as a guide, how could we become better examples of Christ?

Prayer: Have each family member name a person he or she knows who is not a Christian. Through prayer, encourage each other to be better examples of Christ to these specific people.

11.

'50s Night

Focus: God's love is everlasting

Scripture Reference: Jeremiah 31:3

Jeremiah was a Hebrew prophet who warned his people of God's impending judgment. With tears, this "Weeping Prophet" challenged his country to give up its idols and return to God. He reminded the people that no matter the circumstance, God's love for them was everlasting.

God's everlasting love wasn't reserved solely for the ancient Hebrews. It is continued throughout all time. Even when we turn our backs on God today, God's love for us remains. Use this devotion to help your family members learn that God's love will last for their lifetimes—and beyond.

Equipment: You'll need clothes that reflect fashions of the 1950s, and a meal of hamburgers, fries, and soft drinks.

You may also want to use '50s music for fun. Check your local library for tapes or CDs. Use any other '50s memorabilia you have to add to the experience.

Exploration: Several days before you do this devotion, announce to everyone that your family will be celebrating a '50s Night. Encourage each family member to prepare an outfit for the evening. Suggest white T-shirts, rolled-up jeans, and slicked-back hair for guys; skirts, bobby socks, scarves, and ponytails for girls. Younger children may enjoy being dressed as Mouseketeers or as Davy Crockett or Howdy Doody.

Have everyone dress in their '50's fashions just before dinner. When your family arrives in the dining room, serve hamburgers, fries, and soft drinks. For extra fun, play music from the '50s.

After dinner try a few of the following:

- See if anyone can do the jitterbug.
- Watch taped reruns of "Happy Days."
- Sing the theme song from "Davy Crockett."
- See how many items your family can name that hadn't been invented in the 1950s.
- Have your own version of a goldfish swallowing contest—see how many goldfish crackers can be stuffed into a family member's mouth.

Discovery: After everyone has had a taste of life in another time period, ask:

- How are the '50s different from today?
- In what ways are the '50s and today alike?
- If you could pick any era (besides today) in which to live, what time period would you choose? Explain your answer.
- Why do you think God had you be born in this current time period?

Read Jeremiah 31:3 aloud. Tell everyone that these words were meant to comfort people who had turned away from God. God wanted them to know that even though their nation would collapse because they didn't love God anymore, God still loved them. Continue discussion with these questions:

- Why do you think God included this verse in the Bible?
- What would you think if God loved people from the '50s more than God loved us today?
- How does God show love to us even when we don't obey him?
- How do you feel knowing God's love lasts forever, no matter what we do?
- Why is it important that you love others?

Prayer: Have each family member thank God for a specific way they see God showing love to him or her today, such as through a friend, through other family members, through the Bible, or through nature. Have each person also tell how they will love others.

12.

Backwards Night

Focus: Putting others first

Scripture Reference: Mark 9:33-35

Which of us is the greatest? Jesus' followers argued about this question as they walked the road to Capernaum. Perhaps Peter thought he was the smartest while another thought he was better looking. Maybe the fishermen figured they had more status than the tax collector. Yet when Jesus asked what they were arguing about, all of them were embarrassed. Jesus ended the discussion by explaining that those who want to be great should become servants to all.

Being a servant hardly seems to be the way to get ahead in today's society. Yet this is how God wants us to show his love to others and become important in his eyes. Use this devotion to help family members see that being great isn't a matter of intelligence or social status. Rather, it's achieved through being "backwards" and putting others before ourselves.

Equipment: Dinner, complete with salad and dessert

Exploration: Before everyone comes to the dinner table, have them return to their rooms, remove their clothes, and put them back on—backwards. (If something simply will not fit backwards, have the family member wear it inside out.)

When everyone gathers again at the table, begin the meal with dessert. (It's not going to kill you to chow down on the junk first for one night!) Follow with the main course, and finish off with salad. Then sit back and let your food digest as you go through Discovery.

Discovery: Have family members discuss these questions:
▪ Why was it unusual for us to have dinner backwards? What did you like about it? What didn't you like about it?

Read Mark 9:33-35 together, then discuss these questions:
▪ The disciples were arguing about who was the greatest. How did Jesus define greatness?
▪ How was Jesus' definition of greatness "backwards" according to the disciples' expectations? How does Jesus' definition of greatness compare to modern definitions?
▪ Why do you think Jesus said that the greatest of all must be the last of all and servant of all?
▪ When have you seen someone in our family put others first? How did that make you feel about that person?
▪ What makes it hard for you to go last and let others be first? What can you do this week to overcome those obstacles?

Prayer: Let family members know that being backwards tonight meant getting dessert first, but in reality putting others first isn't always a piece of cake. Pray that God will give your family members the desire to put others first at all times.

Then have each family member agree to wear their socks inside-out tomorrow to help them remember that God wants Christians to be "backwards" and serve others instead of fighting to be first.

13.

No Foolin'

Focus: Wisdom and foolishness

Scripture References: Psalm 14:1, Proverbs 9:10-12

In medieval England, fools were simply harmless acrobats out to entertain all who watched them. But thousands of years ago, Israeli history described fools in a much more serious way. A fool was one who refused to believe God existed, and therefore ignored God's wisdom for living.

Today, painted clowns play the roles of the medieval fools, but millions of ordinary people can still be called fools according to the ancient Israeli definition. Chasing after material possessions, popularity, careers, and a host of other temporary things, these fools either ignore or deny God's existence. Use this devotion to show your family how to avoid the foolishness of today's temporary world, and to gain the riches of God's eternal wisdom.

Equipment: A variety of kitchen utensils, newspapers or torn grocery sacks, a family meal, and a Bible

Exploration: Plan an April Fool's Day dinner for your family with the table setting being the foolish part of the event. Don't allow any regular plates, forks, spoons, or knives. Instead, use items such as skillets, plastic lids, or cookie sheets as plates, and give each person at least two utensils (items such as a meat fork, spatula, ice cream scoop, or fondue spear) to use as silverware.

Use newspapers or torn grocery sacks for the table covering. Collect napkins of various colors. Basically, make the table as much of a hodgepodge as possible!

Serve any meal your family enjoys, as long as it requires the use of utensils. Spaghetti or stir-fry are good choices. Hamburgers or pizza are out as they can be eaten with fingers and won't require the hassle of the various utensils.

As your family eats (or attempts to eat), ask the following questions:

- What's the best April Fool's Day prank you ever pulled?
- What's the best April Fool's Day prank someone has pulled on you?
- What would be a fun prank to do if you had a lot of time, money, and help in doing it?

Discovery: Serve dessert. (You can pull out the real forks and spoons now.) While everyone's at the table, read Psalm 14:1 and discuss the following questions:

- Did you feel foolish trying to eat with these utensils? Why or why not?
- How does Psalm 14:1 describe foolish people in this passage?
- Why do you think a fool could be described in this way?

Read Proverbs 9:10-12, then continue the discussion by asking:

- Who is the wisest person you know? Why do you consider this person wise?
- Why do you think this passage says that wisdom begins with respect for God?
- What is one thing we can do this week to show respect for God?

Prayer: Pray for each family member by name, asking God to help him or her live wisely in God's eyes. As you mention family names, give each person a small reminder of what you talked about during this devotion. For example, you might give an odd utensil that you used during the meal, or a slip of paper with Proverbs 9:10 written on it. After prayer, encourage everyone to put their reminders in prominent places in their rooms this week to help them focus on God's wisdom for living.

Disability Dishwashing

Focus: We should help, not hurt, each other

Scripture References: Leviticus 19:14, Ephesians 4:32

In Leviticus 19:14 God gave specific instructions regarding the treatment of disabled people. Respect and kindness were the rule. The Israelites were told not to curse the deaf or purposely trip the blind.

Ephesians 4:32 strengthens the sentiment of Leviticus 19:14 with its encouragement to express love and kindness to others.

While your family may or may not have deaf or blind members, everyone suffers from some kind of disability. One may be a slow learner, another may struggle with impatience, and a third may have poor eyesight. Regardless of the limitation, everyone can treat others with respect, love, and kindness as often as possible. Use this devotion to help your family understand the importance of how they treat one another.

Equipment: A stack of dirty dishes and the equipment to wash them, and a Bible

Exploration: Tell the family that tonight is the dishwasher's night off so everyone will be helping. Decide together who will clear the table, wash, rinse, dry, and put away dishes. (Smaller families can double up on responsibilities. Larger families can have several members doing the same task.)

Before everyone gets started, announce that each person will have to work with a disability during the dishwashing. Assign each family member some kind of disability for the duration of the cleaning. For example, have one person work without speaking, another with her eyes closed, and a third without using his right hand. Make sure each person has at least one handicap. Then work together to get the dishes clean. When the dishes are put away, let everyone resume normal use of their bodies and gather for the Discovery section of the devotion.

Discovery: Discuss the following questions together.
- How did you feel as we washed the dishes?
- How did others help you? Hinder you?
   Read Leviticus 19:14 aloud.
- What would you think of someone who yelled at a deaf person? What about someone who purposely tripped a blind person?
- If you were permanently disabled with the handicap assigned you during the dishwashing, how would you want others to treat you? Why?
- In what ways other than physical handicaps are all people disabled?
   Read Ephesians 4:32 together.
- Who does God want us to show love and kindness to?
- How is being unkind to another family member like tripping a blind person?
- When do you feel mistreated? What kind of treatment makes you feel loved and special?

Prayer: Sit in a circle and have each person think of one weakness he or she struggles with, such as a quick temper, shyness, or difficulty in school. Be sure to include yourself and your own weaknesses. Then have all family members brainstorm ways they can help each other overcome their weaknesses.

Finally, have family members pray for the person on their right, asking God for help in overcoming the weaknesses that person shared.

15.

Kitchen Theology

Focus: Spiritual growth

Scripture Reference: 1 Peter 2:2-3

Imagine what life would be like if no one ever grew up: Diapers everywhere. Formula stains all over the world. An entire population of whining, crying, self-centered people who need someone to care for them, or else they'll die.

In 1 Peter 2:2-3, the apostle tells us to long for the pure and simple teaching of God in the same way that a baby longs for milk. In plain, direct speech, Peter encourages us to use that teaching to grow up in our faith. Use this devotion to help your family understand the importance of an ever-maturing faith.

Equipment: A jar of baby food (any flavor), a bowl of soup, a sandwich, a glass of milk for each family member, and a Bible.

Exploration: Conduct a family taste test using the baby food, soup, and sandwich. When everyone has tasted the foods, let each person tell which food they liked best and why.

Discovery: Read I Peter 2:2-3 and answer the following questions:
■ What would you think of an adult who ate only baby food? Or of parents who fed their baby pizza and cola?
■ Can we live or grow if we ignore eating? How would we feel if we did this?
■ What happens to our faith and acts of love when we ignore God?
■ How can we help each other grow strong in God?

Prayer: Give a glass of milk to each family member. Explain that just as milk helps our bodies grow, God's Word helps our faith grow. Have everyone say this prayer in unison as you "toast" with your milk: "Lord, may this milk we drink now be a symbol of our desire to drink the 'milk' of your Word. Help us to continually grow stronger in faith. In Jesus' name, amen."

16.

The Language of Prayer

Focus: Prayer

Scripture Reference: Romans 8:26-27

"Most Holy Heavenly Father, we thank Thee for Thy bountiful blessings . . ."

Do your prayers ever sound like this? Or are you intimidated when asked to pray aloud because your prayers *don't* sound like this? Romans 8:26-27 provides comfort to those whose prayers are less than eloquent by explaining that the Holy Spirit interprets our prayers to God.

Struggling through foreign words and phrases may remind you of trying to pray with the "right" words. Help your family members see that God hears and understands all our prayers because we have a holy Interpreter.

Equipment: Several foreign language dictionaries checked out from your local library, and a Bible

Exploration: Gather your family and explain that you'd like each person to share a sentence about their day. But this sentence cannot be in English or any other language commonly spoken in your household. Pass out the various language books and have family members interpret their sentences into a foreign language. (Older family members can help younger ones.)

When everyone has done their best to formulate a sentence, take turns trying to express yourselves and understand each other.

If you want to take more time with Exploration, work together looking up and saying various expressions or questions. For example, "We're having dinner at 6:00 p.m. tonight," or "Did you brush your teeth yet?"

Discovery: When everyone is tongue-tied, return to your native language and discuss these questions:

■ If you were to go to a country where one of the languages we experimented with is used, how comfortable would you be talking with others? Explain.

■ Have you ever been in a situation where you couldn't talk with someone because of a language barrier? If so, tell about what happened.

■ In what ways does prayer sometimes seem like a foreign language?

Read Romans 8:26-27 aloud and continue with the discussion:

■ How can we be sure God understands our prayers?

■ If you had an interpreter, how would you feel about going to a country where another language is spoken?

■ How do you feel about praying now that you know the Holy Spirit is your interpreter?

■ What's one thing you'd like other family members to pray about for you this week?

Prayer: In your language books, look up the phrase, "Father, thank you for hearing my prayers." When each person is ready, have everyone pray this prayer aloud at the same time using the language of their books, knowing that God can hear and understand words of every language.

17.

Mirror, Mirror

Focus: Love shows others we're Christians

Scripture Reference: John 13:34-35

On the night before his death, Jesus gave a simple, yet profound, command to his disciples: Love each other. This command recorded in John 13:34-35 also included a promise: The disciples' love for each other would reflect Jesus to the world.

Jesus' command of love holds true for Christ's disciples today. As we love each other, we reflect Jesus to others. What better way for a family to express their love for God than through their actions toward each other! Use this devotion to help your family see the importance of showing love to one another.

Equipment: A large mirror (such as a bathroom mirror or a full-length mirror) or several smaller mirrors; makeup such as eyeliner, lipstick, cream eye shadow, and blush; and a Bible. You may want to purchase inexpensive makeup for this activity—the items will most likely be ruined.

Exploration: Have family members look at themselves in the mirror. Then have everyone apply makeup right on the mirror to transform their reflections into clowns, cowboys, princesses, monsters, and so on. Encourage family members to paint colorful noses, mustaches, eyelashes, hats, and whatever else they can think of. (Younger children may need a little assistance, or can look at their reflections while older family members apply the makeup to the mirror.)

Trade places with each other and see your reflection in another person's drawing. Decide which new reflection each person looks best in.

These temporary makeovers can be left on the mirror for a few days, or washed off as soon as you like. (Use soap and water on an old cloth first, then use window cleaner.)

Discovery: Read John 13:34-35 together and discuss the following questions:
- Jesus loved us, and wants us to show that love to each other. Why? How is loving others a way of reflecting Jesus' love?
- Your reflection in a mirror isn't really you. But if someone were to look at your reflection, what could they learn about you?
- If someone were to judge Jesus' love by the way you show love to your family members, what conclusions would they come up with? Why?
- What's one specific way we can show love to every person in our family this week? How will this reflect Jesus' love?

Prayer: Putting makeup on the mirror changed our reflection, but it didn't change us. Thank God that no matter how poorly we reflect God's love, God is still the same. Ask God to help family members reflect him through their actions this week.

18.

No Place to Hide

Focus: Attributes of God—God is omnipresent

Scripture Reference: Psalm 139:1-12

"You can run, but you can't hide!"

Only one person can make this boast and always back it up—God. As Psalm 139:1-12 eloquently points out, God inhabits every aspect of life. Men, women, boys, and girls can run, but they can never hide from the presence of God.

Your family can take great comfort in knowing that God will never lose track of them. In fact, God will never leave them. When they lie awake at night, God is there. When they are afraid or worried, God is there. When they experience their greatest joys, God is there. Use this devotion to remind your family to take advantage of the power of God's presence.

Equipment: A Bible

Exploration: Gather your family together for a game of "Sardines." This game is similar to hide-and-seek, but in Sardines, only one person hides, and the rest of the family tries to find him or her.

Have everyone go into the same room while the person who is "it" hides somewhere in the house. After waiting two minutes, the family may begin hunting. Whenever someone finds the hidden person, they should hide *with* him or her, remaining until everyone has arrived at the hiding place.

This game can be played at any time of day, but is especially challenging for older children when played in the dark.

Discovery: After several rounds of Sardines, huddle together in the last hiding place and ask your family:
■ What was the best hiding place in our house? Who is the hardest person to find? Who is best at finding others?
   Read Psalm 139:1-12 and discuss:
■ Where can we hide from God? Is there any place that God cannot go?
■ Do you ever try to hide from God? Why? Does it work?
■ When are times you are glad God is always with you?

Prayer: Tell your family that because God is everywhere, God can hear them all pray no matter where they are. Then send family members to different parts of the house for five minutes of silent prayer. Encourage everyone to pray for God to make his presence known each day of their lives.

19.

Paper Airplane Contests

Focus: Attributes of God—God is Creator

Scripture Reference: Ephesians 2:10

Like an admirer at an art gallery, the Apostle Paul speaks proudly of God's creative genius in Ephesians 2:10. God has made us what we are, he says, and the implication is that God certainly doesn't make junk.

Society tells us we need to live up to certain images and expectations, and so we get caught up in a cycle of "if onlys." If only we could be prettier . . . if only we could have more money . . . if only we were smarter . . . if only . . . if only . . . if only. However, your family members can be proud of who they are simply because each one is one of God's masterpieces. Use this devotion to remind them of Paul's words in Ephesians 2:10, "God has made us what we are."

Equipment: Plenty of notebook paper, some small prizes, and a Bible

Exploration: Give each family member several sheets of paper and instruct them to make some paper airplanes.

When everyone has two or three models that they like, have a variety of paper airplane contests. Award prizes for things like the longest flight, the most accurate flight, the most durable plane, the most creatively constructed plane, the funniest flyer, and so on. Be sure each family member wins at least one prize.

Discovery: When the aerial exhibition is finished, discuss these questions:
- How did you feel making your airplanes? Watching them fly?
- How did the airplanes reflect their creators?

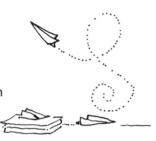

   Read Ephesians 2:10 and ask:
- How do you think God felt when he created you? How do you think God feels watching you "fly" through life?
- How do we as individuals reflect our Creator?
- How long will it be before God is finished constructing us?
- What prizes will there be for us when we finally finish life's race?

Prayer: Have family members take turns saying the prayer below. Have them fill in the blank with one positive quality they like about themselves.

   "God, one thing I like about the way you made me is _____ . Help me to live in such a way as to reflect you, my Creator."

20.

The Name Says It All

Focus: Living up to your name

Scripture Reference: Acts 11:26

   Many people in the Bible are named to reflect their personality, looks, or circumstances surrounding their birth. The Scriptures also use many names for God, each describing one aspect of God's being. In the city of Antioch, the believers were first given a name to reflect their life-styles—Christian, meaning "follower of Christ."

Parents usually put great effort into naming their children. Maybe you named your daughter after your mother, in hopes she will grow to be a woman of character like her grandmother. Perhaps your son's name means "priceless," because you consider him a priceless treasure. Or maybe you want your child to grow up uniquely herself, so you created a brand-new name for her.

Regardless of their given names, anyone who claims to follow Jesus has another name as well—Christian. Use this devotion to encourage your family members to live up to their given names and to the name "Christian."

Equipment: A Bible

Exploration: Sit down with your children and tell them the stories of when they were born. Describe the events during the weeks leading up to their birth, and your feelings about their arrival. Tell your kids how you decided on their names and how their names reflect positive qualities in them. Then have everyone take turns answering these questions:

■ If you had to change your name today, what would you change it to? Why?

■ What do you like best about your name? What do you like least?

■ If you could give your name a new meaning, what would it be? Why?

■ How can you live up to the positive meanings behind your name each day of your life?

Discovery: Read Acts 11:26 together and discuss the following questions:

■ Why do you think people began calling Jesus' followers Christians?

■ What do you think early believers liked most or least about being called Christians?

■ Do you think the name "Christian" means the same thing today as it did during the time of the early church? Why or why not?

▪ How can you live up to the positive meanings of the name "Christian" each day of your life?

Prayer: Thank God for the privilege of being called his followers.

21.

Risky Business

Focus: Making wise choices

Scripture Reference: 1 Kings 3:5-14

1 Kings 3:5-14 recounts Solomon's asking God for wisdom. God gave Solomon, the new king of Israel, the equivalent of one wish. Instead of requesting riches or power, the new king asked for guidance. God was so pleased with this request that he agreed to honor it, and he also gave Solomon wealth and honor.

Wise decision making can be difficult to teach. Not every wise decision is rewarded, and some unwise decisions seem to have benefits. This devotion demonstrates the immediate results of making wise decisions, and leads into discussion of decisions whose results may be more long-lasting.

Equipment: One package of refrigerated sugar cookie dough, sugar, salt, baking pans, utensils, and a Bible

Exploration: As a family, prepare the sugar cookies according to the directions on the package. But before baking the cookies, dip four of the dough pieces into sugar and eight dough pieces into salt. Bake these with the rest of the cookies.

When the cookies are done, secretly mix the sugar-topped and salt-topped cookies together and place them on a plate. Warn family members of the possibility of choosing a salt-topped cookie; then give each person three seconds to choose one cookie. Have everyone bite into their cookie at the same time. (If no one got a salt-topped cookie, have family members keep choosing until at least one person gets "salted.")

Discovery: Allow anyone tasting a salt-dipped cookie to have several drinks of water. Then enjoy the remaining cookies together as you discuss these questions:

■ How did you decide which cookie to choose?

■ What can we learn from the way we chose our cookies that can help us make good choices in real life?

■ Drinking water helps wash away the salty taste of a salt-topped cookie. What can "wash away" the consequences of a bad decision in real life?

Read 1 Kings 3:5-14 together.

■ What decision would you have made in Solomon's situation?

■ Why was God pleased with Solomon's request?

■ How can we please God with our decisions today?

■ How does wisdom affect the choices we make?

■ How do you respond when others seem to be rewarded for making choices that go against what the Bible teaches? Why do you think God allows that to happen?

Tell family members that the consequences of our decisions don't always happen immediately. Then have each person give an example of a decision that may lead to a future reward and an example of a decision that may lead to future disappointment. For example, studying hard in school can bring a future reward of good grades, and treating friends unkindly can bring a future disappointment of losing them.

Prayer: Have each person share a decision he or she is facing right now, no matter how small it may seem. Spend time as a family discussing and thinking through the possible results of the decision. Then have everyone pray for another family member, asking God to give this person wisdom like Solomon's to make the right decision.

22.

Puppet Show

Focus: God gives us physical and spiritual life

Scripture References: Genesis 1:26-27; 2:7, 21-22; John 20:30-31

The passages in Genesis recount the culmination of God's first recorded creative acts, the creation of the first man and woman. The incredible complexity of our bodies demonstrates the creativity and power of God. Doctors still don't understand everything about our physical selves, yet God was able to form the first person as easily as we make a clay figure—maybe even more easily!

God has never stopped creating. Even today God works to give physical life to all living things. In addition, God gives spiritual life to all who believe in him. Is your family aware of their utter dependence on God for their lives? Use this devotion to introduce to them the life-giving power of their awesome Creator.

Equipment: Paper lunch sacks, markers, scissors, glue, scraps of cloth or construction paper, and a Bible

Exploration: It's time to make puppets! Give each family member a paper lunch sack. Spread the craft materials around the table and have each person make a puppet out of his or her sack. Encourage creativity in using fabric and paper scraps to create facial features, hair, even fashionable clothes for each puppet.

When the puppets are complete, work together to make a puppet show using all the puppets. If your family is larger than five, form two groups and have each group perform for the other. Shows could be a reenactment of a favorite fairy tale, Bible story, or an original story. Do as many shows as your family wants.

Discovery: After the shows ask the following questions:
- How did you give your puppet life?
- How is your puppet like you?
  Read Genesis 1:26-27; 2:7, 21-22 together.
- How did God give us life?
- How did God make us like him?
  Read John 20:30-31 together.
- This verse says we can have life by believing in Jesus. When you put your hand into your puppet, you were giving it life. In what ways do you see God's hand giving you life?

Prayer: Have everyone don their puppets. Then have the puppets "pray" for their creators, asking God to help them in specific ways to take full advantage of God's gift of life. Then sing "I've Got a River of Life," or another chorus about life. Have the puppets sing along too.

23.

Hand Shadows

Focus: Knowing God

Scripture Reference: 1 Corinthians 13:12

Wouldn't it be great if we knew all the secret mysteries about God? There would be no more confusion, no misunderstandings, and no wild interpretations of the Bible. But there would also be no faith, no hope for the future, and no reason to pursue knowing God better.

In 1 Corinthians 13:12, Paul reminds us that while we live on this earth we can only glimpse God, as if we're looking at a dim reflection. At times it's frustrating not being able to fathom all of God's mystery, but we can be confident God has revealed all we need to know for now. And we can take hope in knowing that the day will come when we'll see God clearly. Until that day, use this devotion to encourage your family to "shine a light" on their knowledge of God.

Equipment: A flashlight, a hand mirror, and a Bible

Exploration: Go into a darkened room with a blank wall area. Have one person hold up the flashlight while others use their hands to make shadows on the wall. Try to make things such as a rabbit, dog, or flying bird. Take turns making shadows and seeing if others can guess what you're making.

Discovery: Turn the flashlight to the Bible and read 1 Corinthians 13:12. Then talk about these questions:

■ When we were making shadows, what made it difficult to tell what creature was being depicted?
■ What would have made the identity of your creatures more obvious to others?

With the lights still off, have family members look at themselves in the hand mirror.
■ How is a "dim reflection" as mentioned in this verse like a shadow?
■ In what ways do we see only a dim reflection or shadow of what God is like?
■ God sees us clearly, and someday we'll see God clearly too. What would you like to ask God when you're able to see him clearly?

Prayer: Turn the light to the wall again and hold "shadow hands" with each other. (Your hands may not actually be touching, but make them touch in the shadow.)

Have family members pray for those whose shadows they're touching and thank God for one good thing they can see clearly about each other. For example, "Lord, thank you that I can clearly see Mom is an affectionate person," or "Thanks that I don't have to look at a shadow to know Jill has a wonderful laugh."

24.

A Letter for Me

Focus: God knows the future

Scripture Reference: Genesis 37, 39–45

Genesis chapters 37 and 39–45 recount the story of Joseph. Joseph had visions of a bright future for himself—until his jealous brothers sold him into slavery. As the years passed slowly, it seemed Joseph's life was a series of "one step forward and two steps back" experiences. Yet through it all God knew what was ahead for Joseph and used each situation to prepare Joseph for his future.

Like Joseph, we never can be certain what lies ahead. Even when things seem to be going well, circumstances can quickly change our outlook on life. But throughout life, Christians can be sure that the future is still in God's hands. Use this devotion to encourage your family to trust God with the future.

Equipment: Pens, paper, and a Bible

Exploration: Have each family member write a letter addressed to himself or herself. This letter should tell what is happening in the writer's life at this time, and what the writer expects to be doing one year from now. Place all the letters in an envelope and seal it. Tell family members you'll keep the letters in a safe place, to be opened exactly one year from today.

Then ask family members to imagine they had opened letters from last year. Have everyone share what they think "last year's letters" might have said and how those letters would compare to the letters they wrote today.

Discovery: If you have older children, read all of Genesis 37, 39–45. If this is too long a reading, summarize the story, touching on these events in Joseph's life:

1. Joseph's father loved him, but his jealous brothers sold him into slavery.

2. He became the overseer of Potiphar's household, but was then put into jail for a crime he didn't commit.

3. While in charge of all prisoners, he interpreted two dreams correctly, but was then forgotten and left in jail.

4. Finally, he interpreted the king's dream and was made a royal official.

5. During a famine Joseph's brothers came to him asking for food. They didn't recognize him.

6. Joseph forgave his brothers and told them that even though they meant to hurt him, God used everything for good.

   Discuss these questions:

▪ How do you think Joseph felt at the beginning of the story? How do you think he would have felt if he'd known how his future would turn out?

▪ When do you feel like Joseph? Explain your answer.

▪ What makes it hard for you to trust God with your future? Why?

▪ How are you feeling about your life right now? What do you think the future has in store for you?

▪ How can we help each other trust God with our future?

▪ Even though Joseph had hard times, God knew what was ahead and worked everything out. Share about a time when you were discouraged but God worked everything out for the best.

Prayer: Ask God to work in the lives of each family member to bring about God's goals. Also ask for patience as you face the good and bad times ahead.

25.

Down, Down Dominoes

Focus: The choices we make today affect our tomorrows

Scripture References: Genesis 3:1-19, Daniel 3:1-30

These two passages tell two stories of choices. In Genesis 3:1-19, the serpent tempted Eve; she ate the forbidden fruit and Adam quickly followed suit. Both Adam and Eve chose to do the wrong thing. The result? Physical punishment, separation from God, and the beginning of a sin epidemic that lasts to this day.

In Daniel 3:1-30, Shadrach, Meshach, and Abednego were ordered to bow before a statue of the king and worship it. They refused, risking death to do the right thing. The result? A miracle of God and a repentant king.

Every decision yields some result. Even when God forgives our bad choices, we still have to live with the results of those choices. Use these stories to help your family members see the value of making wise choices.

Equipment: A box of dominoes and a Bible

Exploration: When dominoes are set on end within a short distance of each other, knocking down one causes others to fall as well. Work together to set up a boxful of dominoes in long lines on the floor. Then knock down the first domino and watch as all others follow. Try this several times, making a circle, a spiral, and other formations around the room.

Discovery: After making and destroying several domino formations, set the pieces aside. Form two groups. (A "group" can be one person if necessary.) Have one group read Genesis 3:1-19 and the other group read Daniel 3:1-30. (If only one family member is able to read, don't form groups; simply read both stories aloud.)

When everyone has finished reading, have a representative from each group report what happened in the story they read. Then ask the following questions to all:

■ After lining up the dominoes, we pushed one and all the others fell. Why?

■ How is one domino knocking down another and another like the results of making a good or bad choice?

■ What choices did the characters in your stories have to make? What "dominoes were knocked down" because of

the choices your characters made? (Or what were the results of your characters' choices?)
- What choices do you make that can bring good or bad
results?
- When one domino is knocked down, others follow. How
does making good choices help other good choices follow? Is this also true for bad choices? Explain.
- What's the most important choice a person can make?
Why?

Prayer: Have each person think of a choice he or she
made in the past that has resulted in something good. For
example, studying could have the good result of higher
grades, or being kind to a new neighbor could have the
good result of making a special friend. Take turns thanking God for the positive results of these choices, and ask
for wisdom to make good choices in the future.

26.

Bible Story Charades

Focus: The Bible

Scripture References: 2 Timothy 3:16-17 and various other
Scriptures

It holds the medicine for all of life's ailments, yet millions
neglect the Bible's life-giving substance. Often left to collect dust on a shelf, it sits like water ignored in a desert.

2 Timothy 3:16-17 reveals the effects the Bible can have
on people's lives: teaching them about God, exposing sin,
correcting faults, teaching how to live, and helping believers accomplish every good work. Pretty powerful stuff for
a book that usually gets dusted off only on Sundays!

Use this devotion to help your family members recognize
and use the exciting power waiting for them in the pages
of Scripture.

Equipment: Pens and paper, a Bible, and some imagination!

Exploration: Have each family member write down on a slip of paper one or two of their favorite Bible stories along with the appropriate Scripture references. Then take turns acting out the stories you each wrote down while the others try to guess the story.

When a family member draws a slip, have him or her quickly read the story out of the children's Bible before acting it out. (Help younger children by taking them into another room and reading the story aloud to them. Then join in as they act out the story for the rest of the family.) For fun, have a bag of assorted props that each performer can choose from to assist in the acting endeavor. You might include things like hats, sunglasses, a sheet, bandanas, toy swords, pillows, and so on in your bag of props.

Discovery: When everyone has had at least one turn, ask:
■ How did you feel watching the others act out their stories? How did you feel acting out your own?
■ Why did you choose the stories you wrote down? What is something we can learn from each story?
■ Why do you think God included these stories in the Bible?
How would it feel to have lived these stories instead of simply performing them?
■ Read 2 Timothy 3:16-17 aloud and continue discussion.
■ What are other ways besides stories that the Bible shares with us about God and life?
■ How can we encourage each other to read our Bibles?

Prayer: Close with prayer, thanking God for using the Bible to tell us about himself and his love for us.

27.

Gift Day

Focus: Salvation—God's gift of love

Scripture Reference: John 3:16

Arguably the best-known verse in the Bible, John 3:16 sums up the character of God: "God loved the world so much that he gave . . ."

God is still in the giving business. The gift of life through God's Son, Jesus Christ, awaits all who will simply ask and believe. Use this devotion to introduce your family members to the gift that came two thousand years ago, wrapped in flesh, and especially for them.

Equipment: A small gift for each member of the family

Exploration: Announce to the family that it is "Gift Day." Hand each person a small gift you have chosen especially for him or her. When all gifts have been opened and inspected, tell your family that although these gifts were given in love, no present you could ever give would match the gift of love God gave in his Son, Jesus.

Discovery: Read John 3:16 and discuss:
- Why was it important for God to give us Jesus?
- How much did the gift of Jesus cost God? Why does God offer it to us freely?
- How can we accept this gift?
- Do you want to accept God's gift? Why?

Prayer: If any of your family members answer yes to the last question, encourage them to pray asking to receive God's gift of his Son. Before praying, help them understand the need to ask for God's forgiveness and what it means to receive and follow Jesus.

If your family members have already received God's gift, prayerfully sing a song that celebrates Jesus' coming. For example, you might sing "Away in a Manger" or "Thank You Lord for Saving My Soul."

28.

Balloon Bonanza

Focus: Bragging

Scripture Reference: Jeremiah 9:23-24

Kendra boasts about her "A" in spelling, and Scott feels rotten about his "B −." Taylor shows off his skills on the soccer field, and Larry quits in frustration because he'll never be able to compete with Taylor's ability. Although bragging and showing off may make one person feel good, it often makes others miserable.

Jeremiah 9:23-24 warns against bragging. It reminds us that nothing we do can compare to the greatness of God. Use this devotion to help your family understand the dangers of foolish boasting.

Equipment: A bag of 25 or more balloons, string, and a Bible

Exploration: Distribute balloons evenly among family members and have everyone help inflate and tie them. Set aside one balloon to be used during prayer. Then try a few of these games with the rest:
■ See how many balloons each person can stuff into his or her clothing.
■ Use string to tie balloons around your ankles. Have everyone pop each other's balloons by stepping on them, while trying to keep their own balloons from being popped. (To make the game more fair, let younger children tie more than one balloon around their ankles and have older family members use only one balloon.) See who can keep their balloon(s) intact the longest.

- Set a 30-second time limit and see who can pop the most balloons by sitting on them.
- Have everyone lie in a circle on the floor with their feet in the center. Have each family member toss a balloon into the air. Without moving anything but their arms, have everyone keep all balloons from touching the ground for as long as possible. No cheating!

Discovery: Throw away all the balloon shreds, then gather to discuss these questions:
- Have you ever heard the expression "Full of hot air" or "All puffed up"? What do these expressions mean to you?
- How is someone who brags or shows off like a balloon full of hot air?
- What do you think when you hear someone bragging about himself or herself?

   Read Jeremiah 9:23-24.
- What makes you feel like bragging? How do you feel after you show off in front of others? Why?
- Why do you think God warns us not to brag about ourselves?
- What kind of bragging does God like to hear? Why?
- How is a person who brags about God different from a person who is simply full of hot air like a balloon?
- What kinds of actions show that we know and love God?
- What's one thing you will do this week to show others you know and love God?

Prayer: Have family members sit in a circle. Place an inflated balloon in the center of the circle. Suggest that one way to stop bragging is to start showing more love to others. Have family members tell one way they'll show love to the person sitting on their right before the balloon pops or loses its air. For example, "Jenna, I'll feed the dog for you before this balloon pops," or "Dad, I'll give you a hug before this balloon pops."

   Then thank God for each person and ask him to help family members use their breath for loving words and actions instead of bragging.

29.

Comic Creations

Focus: God makes us new

Scripture Reference: 2 Corinthians 5:17

In 2 Corinthians 5:17 Paul sounds a trumpet blast of good news: Those who belong to Christ are new creations! Our past is forgotten! Our present is changed! Our future is made brand-new!

Everyone can look with regret on one aspect or another of the past. Yet, as your family creates something new from something old, they'll get a joyful glimpse at the fresh beginnings promised in 2 Corinthians 5:17.

Equipment: Sunday comics sections saved from several weeks' newspapers, scissors, tape, paper, typewriter correction fluid or tape, pens or pencils, and a Bible

Exploration: Explain to your family that each person will be creating a new comic strip. Then give these directions:
1. Select five frames from a variety of comic strips.
2. Cut out the frames and tape them in a row on a clean sheet of paper.
3. White-out the dialogue with correction fluid.
4. Write new dialogue for the characters in your new strip to create a brand-new story.

The resulting comic strips might have Garfield, Heathcliff, and Hobbes headed on a fishing trip. Or perhaps Blondie can give Cathy some dieting tips. Maybe Dennis the Menace, Calvin, and Dick Tracy will save the world. Encourage madcap creativity and allow family members to work together if they wish.

When all comic strips are completed, pass around the new funnies for everyone to enjoy.

Discovery: Read 2 Corinthians 5:17 aloud and discuss these questions:

■ We took old comic strips and made them new. How is this like what God does to those who belong to Christ?

■ How would you explain the meaning of this verse to a friend?

■ People can tell you've made a new comic strip just by looking at it. How can they tell God has made *you* new?

■ Share one way God is changing you to be like him.

Prayer: Hang all your new comic strips on the refrigerator. After you display each one, thank God out loud for making new creations out of each person in your family.

30.

Music Mania

Focus: The Psalms

Scripture Reference: Psalm 100

The book of Psalms is a songbook containing a wide variety of verse. There are songs of distress, songs of peace and war, songs of comfort, songs of fear, and songs such as Psalm 100 that encourage us to praise God with shouts, service, and singing.

Like the Psalms, music today expresses almost every emotion and thought. As your family shares favorite contemporary songs, they'll also have the opportunity to learn more about the Psalms of centuries ago.

Equipment: Records, cassettes, or CDs and the equipment to play them; a Bible, pencils, and paper

Exploration: Ask family members to come prepared to share their favorite songs. Before playing their songs, have family members share why their songs are their favorites.

As a song is played, ask everyone to listen carefully, even if it isn't his or her style of music. Encourage everyone to try to appreciate what makes this song special to the family member who chose it.

After each song, have each person share his or her thoughts and feelings about the song. Remember to keep the atmosphere friendly. If one person dislikes the favorite song of another, it's okay to share that opinion, but be sure the attitude is kind, not judging.

Discovery: When all songs have been played, discuss the following questions together:

■ How does your favorite song make you feel? What about the song brings out this emotion?

■ What did we learn about each other by listening to our favorite songs?

Tell everyone that the longest book in the Bible, Psalms, is actually a songbook filled with songs expressing a wide variety of emotions. It seems that music was just as important back in Bible days as it is today. Then read Psalm 100 as a sample and discuss these questions:

■ What feeling is the writer of Psalm 100 trying to get across?

■ What do you think the original music to these words sounded like? If you put these words to music, what kind of instruments would you use?

■ What can we learn about the author of this Psalm by reading it? What can we learn about God from Psalm 100?

Prayer: Have everyone write their own psalm or song to God. (Older family members may need to help younger children.) Through these songs let family members express their concerns, praises, thoughts, and feelings to God. If you like, make up tunes to go along with the words. Take turns reading or singing your Psalms aloud.

31.

Joyful Noises

Focus: We can express our joy to God

Scripture Reference: Psalm 150

Psalm 150 encourages us to praise God in a variety of ways, most of which involve noise! The first verses tell what to praise God for, and the following verses describe loud ways to do this.

As your family works together to make noisy instruments during this devotion, reflect on happy sounds: laughter, singing, cheering, encouraging words. Isn't it great to have these sounds directed at you? God must get even greater pleasure out of our happy sounds of praise to him. Use this devotion to help your family make joyful noises just for God.

Equipment: You'll be making a variety of musical instruments from objects around the house. Glasses can be filled with water to various levels and tapped gently with a spoon to make a chime. Oatmeal containers, bowls, pots, and pans make great drums. Foil pie plates smacked together become cymbals. Flutes can be made by blowing over the tops of soda bottles. Rubber bands of different sizes stretched over a shoe box can become a guitar or harp. Make sure you have at least one instrument per family member.

Exploration: Have each family member decide what instrument he or she wants to make. (There can be more than one of the same type.) Suggest the ideas above, or see if anyone wants to create something new. Work together until all the instruments have been completed. See if it's possible to play a tune on any of the gadgets you've created.

Next, have family members take turns naming their favorite praise songs or hymns. (Younger kids may want to choose a nursery rhyme.) "Play" each selection on your musical contraptions, singing and playing with gusto! Bang the drums loudly, strum the guitars enthusiastically, and crash the cymbals! Be sure God really hears you!

Discovery: Read Psalm 150 aloud and discuss the following questions together:
- How does it feel to be praised for something you've done, or for something special about yourself?

- How do you think God felt when we praised him with our home-made instruments?
- If a crowd of people were to gather and praise God as described in this Psalm, what would it sound like?
- Why does God like to be praised with instruments?
- What things can we praise God for doing?

Prayer: Have each person complete the following prayer to God: "God, I praise you because . . ." For example, "God, I praise you because you gave me a great sister." Or, "God, I praise you because you show love to us."

32.

Indoor Olympics

Focus: Running the race

Scripture Reference: Hebrews 12:1-2

Some picture Christianity as a powder-puff religion meant only for people in suits and dresses who sit in a pew once or more a week. The author of Hebrews saw it differently. Hebrews 12:1-2 describes Christianity as a sweaty religion, a way of life meant to be lived just as a race is meant to be run—and won.

Which picture of Christianity does your family have? Use this devotion to help your family members jump in the Christian race.

Equipment: Flatware, a messy bed, couch cushions, toothpaste and family members' toothbrushes, one lace-up shoe from each family member, a stopwatch (or watch with a second hand), a box of Twinkies, and a Bible

Before you begin, you'll need to set up this devotion. Spread out all the flatware (except sharp knives) on the kitchen table. Go to your bedroom and mess up the covers on your bed. Take all the couch cushions off and stack them in a pile on the living room floor. Line up one shoe (with laces untied) from each family member in a row. Last, set everyone's toothbrushes and a tube of toothpaste on the bathroom counter. Now you're ready for your Exploration!

Exploration: Gather the family in the living room and tell them that today is the day of the Indoor Olympics and each person is a competitor. (If you have four or more family members, form teams in order to even out the skill levels.)

The object is to score the best time in the Indoor Olympic Pentathlon. Competitors will be timed to see how long they take to complete all five events. The shortest time wins the Golden Twinkie award.

Here are the five events:
1. Flatware Spelling. Using the flatware, competitors spell out "J-E-S-U-S" on the kitchen table.
2. Couch Repair. Competitors neatly replace the cushions on the couch.
3. Bed Bundling. Competitors neatly make the bed and fluff the pillows.
4. Finger Power. Competitors tie one of each family member's shoes.
5. The Beautiful Bite. Competitors brush their teeth to end the race and stop the clock.

Have the youngest family member go first. (If you're playing as teams, the team with the youngest member goes first.) While this person or team completes the course, other family members can cheer them on or offer words of encouragement. When the first person or team has completed the pentathlon events, stop the clock and reset the supplies for the next competitor(s). Continue until each person or team has completed the course.

After everyone has run the course, award the Golden Twinkie (the first Twinkie out of the box) to the person or team with the quickest time. Then give everyone else consolation Twinkies to eat while you move to the Discovery.

Discovery: Have a family member read aloud Hebrews 12:1-2. Then discuss these questions:
- Did you have a strategy or plan for competing in the Indoor Olympics?
- Did you ever feel like giving up? If so, explain why.
- How is being a Christian like competing in the Indoor Olympics?
- Why do you think the author of Hebrews described the Christian life as a race like our Indoor Olympics?
- What can we learn from the way we ran our pentathlon race that can help us "run the Christian race"?
- What gets in your way as you "run the Christian race"?

Prayer: Lead your family back through the pentathlon course, stopping at the appropriate points to pray prayers similar to the one below.

At the flatware, pray, "Jesus, help us to always see you in even the most ordinary places."

At the couch, pray, "Lord, help us to keep our lives from becoming disorganized."

At the bed, pray, "Lord, make our hearts fresh like a newly made bed."

At the shoes, pray, "Lord, keep our lives on the solid footing of your Word."

At the toothpaste, pray, "Lord, help our mouths to speak your encouraging words to everyone. Amen."

33.

Interior Decorators

Focus: Heaven

Scripture Reference: John 14:2-3

Remember the preparations you made when you found out a new child would be added to your family? Maybe you got a new crib. Perhaps you found a high chair at a garage sale. Or maybe you went all out and redecorated a room.

But nothing you did could ever compare to the preparations Jesus promised to make for us in John 14:2-3. God decorated the universe in only six days. Now he's decorating your family members' places in heaven—and he's been at it for several thousand years. Use this devotion to help your family look forward to seeing Jesus' preparations for their heavenly homes.

Equipment: Your living room and a Bible

Exploration: Gather the family in the living room and tell them it's redecorating time. Get ideas from all family members, then rearrange the furniture to the best of your family's liking. Keep the attitude fun and light as you move the furniture and try new things. (Don't worry, you can always change it back if you don't like it!)

Try out several different options until you arrive at one that satisfies everyone. If you have heavy furniture, you might consider diagramming your ideas before actually moving objects. That will help you picture what the new arrangement might look like.

Discovery: After everything is in its new place, have everyone relax in the living room. Tell your family that just as you prepared this room for comfortable living, Jesus is busy preparing a place for his followers in heaven. Then read John 14:2-3 and discuss these questions:

■ How does it make you feel to know that Jesus is preparing a place for you? Explain.

■ What do you think the place Jesus is preparing for you might be like?

■ Were you ever tempted to give up while we were redecorating? Why or why not?

■ Do you think Jesus will ever give up on you and quit preparing your place in heaven? Why or why not?

■ We know that Jesus is preparing heaven for you, but how is he also preparing you for heaven?

Prayer: Gather the family in a circle and hold hands. Pray a prayer similar to this: "Jesus, thank you for caring enough to prepare a place in heaven for us. Until we get there, please make our home a little bit of heaven here on earth. In your name we pray, amen."

34.

God's Recipe Book

Focus: Finding God's will

Scripture Reference: Psalm 119:105

With 176 verses, Psalm 119 is the longest chapter in the Bible. Verse 105 tells us that God's Word is a guide, showing us the way God wants us to go.

Your kids probably don't rave about the wonderful guidelines you've set and beg you for help in obeying them! But just as following a recipe results in a tasty snack, following the Bible's teaching pleases God and helps us live our lives as loving Christians.

Equipment: Measuring cups and spoons, mixing bowls, a spoon, two six-cup muffin pans, and the ingredients listed in the recipe below. (Don't bring the muffin pans out of the cupboard until they're needed or it will "give away" the recipe.) For this devotion use a King James Version Bible.

Exploration: Explain that you'll be reading a recipe to your family and that they'll need to follow your directions to make a snack. Read the references listed below and have family members look up the verses in a KJV Bible to discover what ingredients to use. The correct ingredients are listed in parentheses to ensure you use the right items!

Mix the following in a large bowl:
- 1¾ cups Leviticus 24:5 (flour)
- ¼ cup Jeremiah 6:20 (sweet cane or sugar)
- 2½ teaspoons Amos 4:5 (leaven or baking powder)
- ½ teaspoon Genesis 19:26 (salt)

In a smaller bowl mix:
- Jeremiah 17:11 (one egg), beaten
- ¾ cup Job 10:10 (milk)
- ⅓ cup Exodus 29:7 (cooking oil)

Add the liquid ingredients to the dry ingredients. Stir until moist. Batter will be lumpy; do not overstir. Grease muffin pans and fill two-thirds full. Bake at 400° F. for 20–25 minutes. Remove muffins from pans, cool, and eat with 2 Samuel 17:29 (honey and butter)!

Discovery: As you wait for the muffins to bake, discuss the following questions:
- When did you guess what we were making?
- What were you thinking as I read the ingredients and directions?
- What made it difficult to follow my directions?
- What kind of a recipe has God given us for life? What ingredients should we put in our lives?

Read Psalm 119:105 together.
- What does this verse say about God's Word?
- How is the Bible like a recipe book for life?
- What's the best way to learn what directions God has for us?
- How can other family members help you follow God's directions for life?

- How will our lives be a blessing for others if we use God's Word as a light and lamp?

Prayer: Serve the finished muffins to your family. As you give each family member a muffin, say a prayer like the following: "Lord, I pray that you'll help (family member's name) to follow the 'recipes' for life written in your Word."

35.

Going Camping

Focus: Depending on God for daily needs

Scripture References: Exodus 13:20-22, 16:13-18, 17:1-7

These passages from Exodus tell of God's miraculous provisions for the Israelites as they camped in the wilderness. God guided the people in the form of a pillar of cloud or fire. God provided food daily in the form of manna and quail. When water supplies ran out, God caused water to come from a rock.

The Israelites weren't always sure that God would provide, and they often complained about their situation. But because they were in such a desperate situation, they were forced to rely on God. In spite of their complaints, God provided day after day, month after month, year after year.

Although most American families don't live in the wilderness, we still have trouble relying on God to meet our needs. Instead of looking to God we look to ourselves, our friends, our church, or our government to take care of us. Yet God wants us to trust him for our daily provisions. Use this devotion to bring home the truth that the same God who cared for the Israelites thousands of years ago cares for your family today.

Equipment: Camping supplies. If you don't own and can't borrow a tent, make one by draping blankets, sheets, or tablecloths over chairs. You'll also need blankets or sleeping bags, flashlights, a candle and matches, marshmallows and forks, and a Bible.

Exploration: Announce to your family that tonight you're going camping—in the back yard or a public park. (No fair using a camper or motorhome, as its comfort will detract from the focus of the devotion.)

Gather the items you'll need and head outside to set up your tent. Outside the tent, with careful adult supervision, roast marshmallows over a candle and tell stories. Listen to and identify the night sounds. Decide what the perfect camping vacation would be for your family. Imagine what noises you'd hear if you were actually camping in the wilderness. Then turn on a flashlight and gather inside the tent for Discovery.

Discovery: Read aloud Exodus 13:20-22, 16:3-18; and 17:1-7.

Discuss the following questions together:
- How does our camping experience compare to the Israelites'?
- How did God provide for the Israelites?
- How would you like it if God directed you the same way he directed the Israelites? Would you follow? Explain your answers.
- What do you think manna tasted like? (Exodus 16:31 will give you a clue.)
- How does God provide for you? How do you feel when you're waiting for God to provide?
- What can we learn about trusting God from the way God treated the Israelites?
- What's one area in which we need to trust God more as a family?

Prayer: Have each family member thank God for one convenience they would hate to be without, such as plumbing, microwave ovens, or cars. Ask God to help each family member learn how to rely on God in the days ahead. Then pray for the homeless people in your community and around the world who are forced daily to live without any of the comforts and conveniences of home.

36.

Family Business

Focus: Using our resources to serve God and others

Scripture Reference: 1 Timothy 6:6-10

Society tells us to "look out for number one," to "get while the getting's good," and "the one who dies with the most toys wins." But the message of 1 Timothy 6:6-10 goes against the grain of this type of thinking.

Instead of giving all to gain wealth and possessions, Christians are instructed simply to be content with what they have. Serving God wholeheartedly brings its own everlasting rewards. Use this devotion to give your family an opportunity to serve God by serving others.

Equipment: Materials for a garage sale, and a Bible

Exploration: It's time for a garage sale! Work together to gather items that your family no longer needs or uses. Price them, and set up a sale in your driveway and garage. (If you live in an apartment complex or another area where a sale of this kind is prohibited, reserve space at a nearby weekend flea market or swap meet.) Don't forget to advertise!

As you prepare for this sale, let everyone know the money made from the sale will be donated to a charity. Decide together on one or two persons or organizations to receive this donation. Also determine where unsold items will be donated. Then hold the sale.

Enjoy your time together during the sale. Share the responsibilities of setting up, selling, and cleaning up, so everyone is included. Be sure to offer refreshments and a relaxed, happy atmosphere.

After the sale, deliver unsold items and the financial receipts to your designated charities.

Discovery: When everything has been put away, read 1 Timothy 6:6-10 and discuss these questions:
■ How did it feel to know you wouldn't be getting the money from the sale of your belongings?
■ How does it feel knowing others will benefit from our sale?
■ What kind of "riches" do you think serving God brings?
■ How can loving money and possessions affect your relationships with God and others?
■ How can using money and possessions to serve God and others change your relationships with them?
■ What are other ways our family can serve God with our resources?

Prayer: Have each person think of one belonging they donated to the garage sale. Then have family members take turns praying that God will use those items in a special way to show others God's love.

37.

Watermelon Wonders

Focus: Spiritual growth

Scripture Reference: Mark 4:26-29

This parable compares spiritual growth to the growth of a seed. We don't actually see a plant grow, yet we recognize its developing changes and appreciate its fruit. In the same way we may not actually see ourselves grow spiritually, but we can recognize changes in our lives and look forward to being harvested into God's eternal home.

Equipment: An outdoor area, several watermelons, a large knife, and a Bible

Exploration: Have a family party based on a watermelon theme. Go into your backyard or a local park, cut open the watermelons and let the fun begin! Try the following activities:
- See who can spit a seed the farthest.
- See who can pinch a wet watermelon seed and shoot it the farthest.
- Cut wedges of equal size and have a watermelon eating contest. No hands allowed!
- Create hats out of the rounded ends of watermelon rind. Who has the most fashionable helmet?
- Cut round sections and eat out the middle. Then use the round rind sections in a ring-toss game.

Discovery: Wash up. (Get out the hose!) Then gather to discuss these questions:
- What's the biggest watermelon you've ever seen? How much do you think it weighed?
- Look at a watermelon seed. How can such a huge fruit grow from such a small seed?
  Read Mark 4:26-29 together.
- Can you actually see a plant growing? How can you tell that it's grown?
- What does "spiritual growth" or "growing in Christ" mean? How does it happen?
- If you were to describe your faith in terms of a watermelon seed, at what stage of the growing process would you be in?
- How do you see yourself growing spiritually?

Prayer: Write the word "WATERMELON" down the side of a sheet of paper. Work together to think of one word or phrase beginning with each letter of "watermelon" that represents some way we grow spiritually or that shows evidence of spiritual growth. For example, W could be "worship," A could be "Always showing love," and so on. When the acrostic is complete, ask God to help your family be more like watermelons!

38.

Up a Tree

Focus: God loves everyone

Scripture Reference: Luke 19:1-10

Zacchaeus, a tax collector, wasn't known for his honesty. He was a regular cheat! When Jesus stopped under the tree where this short man had climbed for a better view, everyone was surprised. Zacchaeus couldn't believe Jesus was interested in him, and others couldn't believe Jesus would talk with, even eat with, a sinner.

There are plenty of undesirable sinners in the world today. It's tempting to turn up our noses and say we're better than they are. But Jesus died for all the crooks, criminals, liars, and cheaters too. And they'll never learn about Jesus' power to change their ways unless we show them Jesus' love.

Equipment: A Bible

Exploration: Go outside and climb trees together! (If you don't have a tree large enough to climb, go to a local park and climb the jungle gym.) See how high you can all get; then view the world from a higher perspective. What can you see? Are there enough leaves to hide you from those below? What would be fun to do in a tree?

Discovery: From your perch above ground, read Luke 19:1-10 together and discuss these questions:
■ What's it like being too short to see above others? When is this really annoying?

■ Zacchaeus did a lot of wrong things. Everyone knew he took money that didn't belong to him. Why do you think he was so interested in seeing Jesus that he'd climb a tree?

■ Why were people complaining that Jesus was staying at Zacchaeus' house?

■ What did Zacchaeus do after spending time with Jesus? How did Jesus respond to him?

■ Do you know any people like Zacchaeus? Who are they, and why do they need to know God?

■ When are we like Zacchaeus?

■ How can we show Jesus' love to people like Zacchaeus?

Prayer: Have each family member pray for one person they know who needs Jesus. Ask God to give you opportunities to show love to these persons and introduce them to God.

39.

Mudslingers

Focus: Taming the tongue

Scripture Reference: James 3:5-12

In James 3:5-12 tongues are compared to fire. Just as one tiny flame can start a forest fire, a few words can cause incredible pain and damage.

Name-calling, bragging, put-downs, and other forms of verbal abuse are common in families, especially among brothers and sisters. This devotion can help your family see how hurting others with words is like covering them with filth. Use this devotion as an encouragement for family members to use words to build up, not tear down.

Equipment: A bucket of mud and a Bible

Exploration: Gather outside around a washable item. This could be a wall, tree trunk, or the family car. Ask family members to think of three put-downs or names they hate to hear others use. As each person shares, have him or her scoop up a handful of mud and throw it at the selected item.

When everyone has shared, wash hands and gather around the mud-covered item for Discovery.

Discovery: Read James 3:5-12 aloud and talk about these questions:

■ How do the words you shared make you feel when you hear others say them?

■ How are those put-downs like the mud we just threw?

■ What "muddy messes" do unkind words leave on their hearers?

■ Why do you think James 3:5-6 describes our tongues as rudders and fires?

■ Why do you think people put each other down and speak unkindly to one another?

■ If mean words are like mud and fire, what might kind words be like?

■ Based on James 3:5-12, how do you think God wants us to speak to each other?

Pull out a hose and wash the muddy object together. As you work, use your words to build each other up. Give each person the opportunity to share one thing they like about every other family member.

Prayer: Have each family member ask God for help in controlling his or her tongue. Close by thanking God for the opportunity to encourage each other, and asking for help in doing this.

40.

Non-Slumber Party

Focus: Being ready when Christ returns

Scripture Reference: Matthew 25:1-13

Matthew 25:1-13 relates Jesus' parable of ten brides-maids. Jesus compared these ten bridesmaids waiting for their groom to us waiting for his return. All bridesmaids had lamps, but only half prepared for the wait by bring-ing enough oil to keep their lamps lit through the night. The result? Five were ready for the bridegroom's return, five weren't.

While we await the arrival of a special friend, we make preparations for meals, outings, and memorable moments together. In the same way we should be preparing for Christ's return. Use this devotion to help your family mem-bers understand the importance of always being ready for Christ's return.

Equipment: Snacks, games, and other items necessary for a slumber party

Exploration: Invite another family to join yours for a slum-ber party. The theme of the evening is "being awake and ready when Christ returns." Since slumber parties rarely involve sleep, it's a perfect time to practice!

Try some of these events:

■ Sponsor a "Best Snore" contest. Award prizes for loud-ness, originality, and longest snore.

■ Have a pajama fashion show.

■ Tell a "Never-Ending Bedtime Story" where one person begins a story, then taps another person who continues it. See how long you can keep an interesting plot going!

■ Have a pillow fight (or two or three).

■ Have a "Morning Face" contest where everyone messes up his or her hair and tries to look as if freshly awakened.

- Have a "Kids Style the Parents' Hair" time.
- Make "S'mores" over the kitchen stove or in your fireplace. Toast marshmallows on long forks, then sandwich them between graham crackers with a piece of chocolate included as well.
- Play Monopoly, Risk, or another lengthy game.

Discovery: Sometime during this evening of sleeplessness, gather everyone together, read Matthew 25:1-13, and then discuss these questions:

- Who do the foolish bridesmaids represent? What about the wise bridesmaids? The groom?
- Which character in this parable is most like you? Why?
- What does this parable tell us about Jesus' coming return?
- How can we be preparing for Jesus' return like the bridesmaids prepared for the bridegroom?
- What distracts us from preparing for Jesus' return? What can we do about it?

Prayer: Just before you finally go to bed, have everyone gather for nighttime prayers. Have members of both families take turns reciting their favorite prayers from years gone by (such as "Now I lay me down to sleep" or "God bless Mommy and Daddy"). End the prayer time by asking Jesus to help keep you alert and ready for his return, and to live lives of love while waiting.

41.

Picnic Provisions

Focus: Giving

Scripture Reference: John 6:1-14

This passage is John's account of the feeding of the five thousand. People had followed Jesus into an area where no food was available, and now they were hungry. Only one small boy had brought along his lunch: five biscuit-sized loaves of bread and two small fish. Yet Jesus turned this meager offering into a meal for over five thousand people.

What do we have that God doesn't already have? We may feel what we have to offer is insignificant to God. There are so many others with better qualifications, more money to give, more experience, and so on. But in this story we see Jesus using a tiny gift from a child to meet the needs of thousands. Use this devotion to help your family members understand the importance of their gifts.

Equipment: Prepare sandwiches and other picnic foods, and gather items needed for a picnic. (Don't forget the Frisbee!) You'll also need a Bible.

Exploration: Visit a nearby park and enjoy time together playing catch, swinging, and chasing your Frisbee. Then gather together for a picnic. Pass out plates, but give only one person any food. Keep all other provisions put away.

Wait a couple of minutes to see how everyone responds. Should the sandwich be shared? Or does everyone demand the rest of the food be brought out?

Discovery: Pass out the rest of the food, then discuss the following questions as you eat:
■ What would you have done if there really was only one sandwich?
Read John 6:1-14 aloud.
■ How did Jesus use the gift of this little boy?
■ If you had been in that huge, hungry crowd, how would you have felt when you realized there was no food to eat? How would you have felt when Jesus' friends started passing out the food?
■ The boy in this passage gave his lunch to Jesus. What gifts can you give to God? How can God use those gifts?

■ What gifts (not related to money) do each of us give the rest of the family? How does God use those gifts to build up our family?

■ Just as Jesus gave this food to others besides his "family" of disciples, we can give to others outside of our family. What gifts can we offer to people in our community, church, school, or other places?

Prayer: Have each family member thank God for two other family members. Thank God for what these people offer to the family as well as what they offer to God.

42.

Tire Games

Focus: Being used by God

Scripture Reference: Numbers 22

Numbers 22 tells an unusual story about a wayward prophet and a donkey preacher. The prophet Balaam was tempted by Israel's enemies to curse his own people, the Israelites. In order to stop him, God took drastic measures. God sent an angel to kill Balaam on his way to the enemy camp. But Balaam's donkey saw the angel and refused to move. Balaam was furious until God opened the donkey's mouth and allowed it to tell Balaam the error of his ways.

God doesn't normally use donkeys to accomplish his purpose; he uses people. Are your family members available for God to use? Or, like Balaam, are they too busy rushing headlong into the enemy camp? Use this devotion to show your family that they can be used by God.

Equipment: An old tire (check a junkyard), an outdoor area, and a Bible

Exploration: Take your family and an old tire to an outdoor area, such as a backyard or park. Tell everyone their goal is to invent new games a family can play using a tire—and your family is going to test them.

Have family members spend a few minutes brainstorming and experimenting with the tire. Tell everyone to think of unusual ways to use the tire and to build a game around it.

For example, you might play Tree Target Practice, where you stand a certain distance from a tree and try to roll the tire into it. Or you could have Tire Bouncing Races where everyone takes turns sitting on the tire and bouncing it through an obstacle course—best time wins. Or you might lay the tire on the ground and use it as the hoop for a game of basketball. Be creative, and encourage your family members to be creative as well.

After you've got some good ideas, have everyone try out a few. Play as many and as long as you like.

Discovery: After you're all worn out, form a circle around the tire and discuss these questions:
■ What did you think when I told you our goal was to invent new games using a tire?
■ What are other ways people use tires?
■ In what ways are people similar to tires?

Read or tell the story of Balaam from Numbers 22. Then tell your family that although it's unusual to use a tire for games, it's even more unusual for God to make a donkey talk! Continue your discussion with these questions:
■ Which character in this story do you relate to most? Why?
■ Why do you think God used a donkey to correct Balaam?
■ How can God use us to accomplish his goals like he used Balaam's donkey, or like we used our tire?
■ What keeps us from being used by God? How can we overcome those obstacles?

Prayer: Have family members take turns standing inside the tire as you pray a prayer like this for each person: "Lord, we ask you to use (person's name) in new and creative ways to make a difference for Jesus each day of his/ her life. In Jesus' name, amen."

43

Flip of the Coin

Focus: God's direction

Scripture Reference: Jeremiah 29:11

Jeremiah sent a letter to his countrymen who'd been taken away as slaves to Babylon. In the letter Jeremiah revealed startling news for these captives: God had plans for them—plans for good, plans of hope for the future.

In a spiritual sense, all Christians live as temporary captives in a world that's forsaken God. Yet, in spite of life's uncertainties, God still has plans for his followers—and those plans are still good and full of hope. Use this devotion to comfort your family with the news that God's plans are not arbitrary, like the toss of a coin.

Equipment: A coin, a car, and a Bible

Exploration: Pile into the family car. (This can also be a walking adventure, or a coin could be flipped at various stops along a bus route.) Explain that you'll be going on a coin-toss adventure. Have a family member flip a coin. If the result is "heads," you'll turn to the right at the next intersection. "Tails" means a turn to the left. After each turn, have another family member flip the coin to determine which direction you'll go at the next intersection. (Flipping in advance gives the driver time to get into the correct lane for turning.) This could mean driving around the block a few times before getting out of the neighborhood!

Drive for a half hour or so and see where you end up. If you're near a fast-food outlet, stop for soft drinks and ask the Discovery questions there. If not, begin your discussion on the drive home.

Discovery: Discuss the following questions together:
■ What was fun about this trip? What was frustrating?

- What would it be like to make all decisions in life by flipping a coin? Would you be able to plan for the future?
Have someone not driving read Jeremiah 29:11 aloud.
- How does it feel to know God has good plans for your future?
- How can knowing that God is in control of the future help you today?
- What good things do you hope God has planned for your future?

Prayer: Give each family member the opportunity to flip the coin once more. Have those getting "heads" thank God for one good thing God has already done for your family. Have those getting "tails" ask God for guidance as your family moves into the future together.

44.

Mall Watchers

Focus: God looks at our hearts

Scripture Reference: 1 Samuel 16:6-7

1 Samuel 16:6-7 relates Samuel's search for God's appointed king of Israel. Samuel went to the home of Jesse and saw Jesse's son, Eliab, a tall and handsome young man. Samuel saw Eliab's good looks and was sure that Eliab was the man God had chosen. But God had other plans. Samuel judged by outward appearance. God was examining the heart, and he chose Eliab's younger brother, David.

Just as Samuel set great store on physical appearances, people today often "judge a book by its cover." But it's what's inside that makes us special to God. Use this devotion to help your family see the importance of a beautiful heart and life of love.

Equipment: A Bible

Exploration: Take your family to a local shopping mall. Find an empty bench and sit together watching as people walk by. Judging only by their appearances, try to determine the following things about the people you see:
- a person's occupation
- a person's favorite music group
- a person's taste in food
- most likely vacation spot a person would go to

Have family members take turns selecting new passers-by to discuss quietly. Continue until each family member has had a turn.

Discovery: Discuss these questions together:
- How much can you really tell about a person by his or her appearance?
- Do people ever make false assumptions about you based on your looks? How do you know? How does this make you feel?

Read 1 Samuel 16:6-7 together. Summarize what happened.
- What does "heart" mean in this verse? What can God tell about people by looking at their hearts?
- How can we improve our hearts? Which is more important to work on, our hearts or our bodies?
- What is one thing you can do this week to help your heart be more attractive to God?

Prayer: Have each family member pray for the unknown person they selected earlier. Tell them to pray silently for that person's heart. Then pray aloud that God will help family members as they work to make their hearts more attractive to God.

45.

Discount Dilemmas

Focus: We're valuable to God

Scripture Reference: Romans 5:6-8

In a few short words, Romans 5:6-8 sums up the totality of God's love for us. We were God's enemies overcome by sin. Our attitudes and our actions rated hatred and punishment. We should have been worthless to God, but we were not. In fact, God valued us so highly that he gave his Son to die in our place.

At times, everyone in a family must deal with feelings of unimportance and poor self-image. But anyone for whom Christ died is far from unimportant—he or she is priceless! Use this devotion to remind your family members of their incredible worth to God.

Equipment: Two envelopes that each contain $2.67, a copy of the hunt list, two watches, and a Bible

Exploration: Take your family to a large discount department store. In the parking lot, form two teams. (A "team" can be one person if your family is small. Larger families may want to form three teams.) Give each team an envelope containing exactly $2.67, and a copy of the hunt list below.

HUNT LIST

1. Something red
2. A toy
3. A kitchen utensil
4. Something sweet
5. Something smaller than the fist of the youngest team member
6. Something round
7. A gardening item

8. An item used in schools
9. Something that could be worn
10. An item made of paper
11. Something in a can
12. Something soft
13. An item the same color as the hair of the oldest team member

Prepare teams for a shopping scavenger hunt by explaining the rules as follows:

1. Each team has twenty minutes to find and purchase as many items that fit the descriptions on the hunt list as possible. This includes time spent waiting in line to pay for items. All team members should meet back at the car by the arranged time.

2. The team whose purchased items fit the most descriptions on the hunt list is the winner. A purchased item may fit more than one description on the list. For example, red jelly beans could be both something red and something sweet.

3. Only the money in the envelope may be spent, nothing more. Receipts must be kept to verify the amount spent. Tax must be included in the amount spent.

Remind everyone of the correct meeting time, and begin the hunt! When everyone meets at the car after twenty minutes, have each group present its purchases and tell how the purchased items fit descriptions on the hunt list. Congratulate the winners and divide the "loot" as desired.

Discovery: As you drive home, discuss the following questions:

■ What were you thinking during our bargain shopping experience? Why?

■ What made the items we purchased valuable to us? Would you have bought any of these items if they weren't on your hunt list?

■ How do people normally determine what an item is worth? How do we determine a person's worth?

■ Have someone who isn't driving read Romans 5:6-8 aloud.

- What do these verses say about how much we're worth?
- Why do you think Jesus chose to die for us, even when we didn't deserve it?
- How does hearing you're valuable to God make you feel? Explain.
- How can we treat ourselves and others as God's treasures this week?

Prayer: Have everyone take turns praying the following prayer, completing the sentence about another family member: "God, thank you for (name of family member). One thing valuable about (person's name) is (a positive quality about that person)." For example, "God, thank you for Anthony. One thing valuable about Anthony is his cheerful smile." Or "God, thank you for Jane. One thing valuable about Jane is her willingness to help me with my homework."

Be sure each family member is recognized.

46.

Fore!

Focus: The golden rule

Scripture Reference: Matthew 7:12

First-century Jews were consumed with following every nuance of Old Testament law. But in their legalistic zeal they had missed out on the meaning behind the words. So, Jesus summed up the entire Old Testament law with his now famous advice: "Do to others what you want them to do to you."

Families, too, can become consumed with all the "rules" of Christian living. Our kids memorize all the "dos" and "don'ts" but miss out on the simple meaning of God's instruction in the Scriptures. Use this devotion to help your kids break the bond of legalism by helping them understand Jesus' "golden rule" found in Matthew 7:12.

Equipment: A miniature golf course, a Bible, paper, a pen, and a golf ball

Exploration: Take your family to a local miniature golf course. If your family has six or more members, form two groups. Families of five may need to add an extra column on their score card.

Explain to your family that they'll be playing this game with a new set of rules. They are:

1. Each person in the group hits his or her ball. Then the youngest person selects the ball closest to the hole and knocks it in (taking as many swings as necessary). The second-youngest person hits the ball now closest to the hole, and so on, until all balls are in the hole. Write down the number of swings each person took.

2. "Creative" shots are allowed. For example, Dad may form his feet into a V near a difficult hole so a younger family member can more easily make the shot. Or someone may choose to make a shot using the club as a pool cue instead of swinging. In other words, "cheating" (helping) is allowed.

3. As you move from hole to hole, let family members take turns inventing new rules to be followed for that hole only. For example, on the fourth hole, Jamal may require each person to hit left-handed. On the next hole Aisha may ask that each person stand on one foot while swinging his or her club.

4. Afterward, tally up all scores. (If your family needed to form two or more groups, join together again.) Subtract the age of the oldest person from the score of the youngest person, the age of the second-oldest person from the score of the second-youngest person, and so on. In families with an uneven number of players, one member will subtract his or her own age from his or her score. The lowest score wins!

Discovery: If the course offers a pleasant sitting area, gather there. Otherwise discuss the following questions when you arrive at home.

- What would you say was the "golden" rule or most important advice about playing miniature golf in our family?

Explain to family members that as you played, you all created rules to help everyone enjoy the game more. Then point out that two thousand years ago Jesus gave his followers advice that has since become known as "the golden rule" of life.

Have a family member read Matthew 7:12 aloud. Then discuss these questions:

- How did our rules help us enjoy our golf game?
- How might following the advice of Jesus' "golden rule" help us enjoy our family relationships more? What about relationships outside of our family?
- Why do you suppose Jesus' advice in Matthew 7:12 has become known as "golden"?
- How do you want others to treat you this week? What's one thing you can do to treat someone that way this week?

Prayer: Have family members sit in a triangle shape on the floor (an uneven triangle is fine!). Roll a golf ball to another family member in the triangle. When that person catches it, pray a prayer like this for him or her: "Lord, help (family member's name) treat others as he (or she) wants to be treated this week. Help me to encourage (family member's name) as he (or she) lives for you. In Jesus' name, amen."

Have the person holding the golf ball roll it to a new family member and repeat the process.

47.

Photo Finish

Focus: Remembering God

Scripture Reference: Psalm 71:17-18

Psalm 71 is the prayer of an elderly psalmist looking back on his youth and forward to his remaining days. In verses 17-18 the psalmist remembers what God has taught him in earlier years, and promises to tell others what he knows about God. From his past, he gives others insight for the future.

Your family will have many moments worth remembering in the years to come. They'll relive the past joys and pains, successes and failures. The psalmist remembered his past to strengthen others for the future, and your family can do the same. Use this devotion to make a memory with your family today.

Equipment: A camera, roll of film, inexpensive photo album, pen, paper, and a Bible. Cut the paper so it will fit into the photo album.

Exploration: Take your family on a photo adventure, going to various locations and taking pictures of each other. Take turns snapping shots so everyone gets into the pictures, or ask bystanders to take your picture whenever you can.

Have family members suggest locations for funny photos. You may even want to take along some silly props such as hats, wigs, stuffed animals or other toys. In each shot capture the adventuresome spirit of your family. Here are some ideas to get you going:
- At a local park, hanging from the trees.
- In your laundry room, with the smallest family member peeking out of the dryer.

- At the library, having everyone tiptoe in with their fingers to their lips in a "Shhh!" expression.
- Cramming into a phone booth, or having each person talking on a different phone in a line of booths.
- Beside a sporty car at a used car lot.

When you've finished the roll, take it to a one-hour photo developing store. As you wait for the results, complete the Discovery section of this devotion.

Discovery: Discuss the following questions together:
- Years from now when we look back at the pictures we've just taken, what do you think we'll remember?
- If you were to use these pictures to tell one of your future children or grandchildren about our family, what would you tell them?

Read Psalm 71:17-18 together.
- This song was written by an older person who remembered what God had done for him in the past and wanted to pass on these memories to younger people. What's something God has done for you in the past? Do you tell others about this?
- How can remembering what God has done in the past help us now and in the future?

Tell everyone to think about what God is doing in their lives right now. Have them write their answers to the next question before sharing responses with everyone. (Have older family members help ones who aren't able to write yet.)
- What are you learning about God that you want to remember in the future?

Date the pages that have answers to the last question and put them in the front of the photo album. After laughing over your photos, place them in the album and use it in the future to remember the fun outing you had together, and how God has been involved in your lives.

Prayer: Have family members choose one photo that shows something special that they like about your family.

Then have family members take turns praying for God to help your family show those qualities to others.

48.

Remember Me

Focus: Being remembered as a follower of Christ

Scripture Reference: Acts 9:36-42

Tabitha, whose Greek name was Dorcas, was an early follower of Christ known for her good deeds. She died suddenly at the same time Peter was passing through her town. In her home, the widows of the town showed Peter the clothes Tabitha had made for them. Peter prayed over the woman, and she returned to life.

During her life, and even after her death, Tabitha was remembered for putting her faith into action. How will your family members be remembered? Use this devotion to show your family how to be remembered like Tabitha.

Equipment: Paper, pencils, and a Bible

Exploration: Take your family to a local cemetery. Walk through the markers and monuments, taking time to read the engravings. How were these people remembered by their families and friends? Have each family member share a few words they'd like to have on their tombstone. Tell each person one positive thing you'll always remember him or her for. (Other family members can join in the affirmation as well.)

Discovery: Read Acts 9:36-42 aloud and discuss the following questions together:
■ What words do you think Tabitha's friends would have put on her tombstone? Why?
■ How did Tabitha put her faith into action during her life?

- How are you putting your faith into action? How is your family doing this together?
- What do you think people will remember you and your family for?
- What's one thing your family can do this week to put your beliefs into action?

Prayer: Give each family member a sheet of paper and a pencil. Have everyone draw a tombstone. Then have family members compose a one-sentence prayer asking God to help them apply what they've learned during this devotion. Tell everyone to write their prayers on their "tombstones."

For example, a person might write, "Lord, help me show my faith in you this week in the way I talk to my friends." Then take turns praying these prayers out loud.

49.

Grocery Gifts

Focus: Service—Making a difference in your community

Scripture References: Deuteronomy 24:19-21; Matthew 25:34-40

Deuteronomy 24:19-21 reveals much about God's concern for the poor. God not only commanded the ancient Israelites to care for the needy, but gave specific instructions on how to go about it. In Matthew 24:34-40 Jesus makes it clear that when we care for those in need we're showing our love to Jesus.

Does your family share God's concern for the needy? Do family members know specific ways to reach out to those who need help? Use this devotion to reveal God's concern for the poor and practice caring for those in need.

Equipment: Money for a trip to the grocery store, a list of groceries needed for a meal, a map of your city or community, and a Bible

Exploration: As a family, plan a nutritionally balanced meal of your favorite items. Prepare a list of the foods needed to make this meal. When the list is complete, go to a store and buy the listed items.

Take the food to the home of a family you have chosen that is in need of some food. Leave it on their doorstep with an anonymous note explaining why you have left the food. If there are perishable items, call the family when you get home to let them know that there is a gift on their doorstep.

As you return home, talk about how it feels to help others. Thank God for the food he has provided for your family.

Discovery: Read Deuteronomy 24:19-21. Use these questions as discussion starters:

■ How did you feel when we went shopping for the other family? How did it feel after we had shared our food with them?

■ What is God telling us to do here?

■ Why is God concerned with orphans, widows, and the poor?

Read Matthew 25:34-40 and continue your discussion.

■ To whom are we showing love when we care for those in need? How does this make you feel about helping others?

■ What are needs people have other than food? When might someone temporarily need help?

■ How can we continue to show God's love to those in need?

Prayer: Take out the map of your area and divide it into sections equal to the number of people in your family. Give each family member one section. Have everyone pray silently for one minute for the needy people that live in the area on their map portions. Afterward, have family members hang their sections of the map in a prominent place in their rooms as a reminder to pray for the needs in your community.

50.

Pound Puppies

Focus: Jesus' redemptive work

Scripture References: Romans 3:23, 6:23, 10:10-13

These passages in Romans give good news for bad times: Jesus saves. Yes, this phrase seems trite and over-used now, but look at it again, as if you were seeing it for the first time

Jesus saves.

Do you feel the power of those two words? Do you sense the hope of knowing that Jesus does indeed save? Does your family know that Jesus can save them from sin? from death? from the rotting, corrupting power of the devil? Maybe it's time you used this devotion to remind them.

Equipment: A local animal shelter, a willingness to adopt a pet, and a Bible. Note: This devotion may not be appropriate for young children.

Exploration: Take your family on a tour of a local animal shelter. If possible, call ahead and see if you can arrange for an employee there to show your family around and explain his or her work. If that's not possible, explain the work of the shelter yourself, pointing out that any pets not claimed or adopted are eventually put to death.

During the tour ask your family members these questions:
- How does being here make you feel? Why?
- What would you be feeling if you were one of the animals in this shelter?

After the tour, announce to your family that they can rescue one pet and adopt it from the shelter. Let the family choose their favorite and take it home.

Discovery: When you get home, gather the family around the new pet and a Bible. Read aloud Romans 3:23 and 6:23a. Then discuss these questions:

■ How does sin make us feel like caged animals in an animal shelter?

■ How does it make you feel to know that we all deserve death because of our sins?

   Read Romans 6:23b and 10:10-13 before asking the next questions:

■ How did you feel when I said we could rescue this pet?

■ How is the way we rescued this pet like the way Jesus rescues us from sin?

■ Now that we've been rescued, how can we trust Jesus for our everyday needs like this pet will be trusting us?

   Tell your family that although you were only able to save one pet, Jesus is able to save all people from sin.

Prayer: Because your pet is a living symbol of Jesus' redemptive power, have your family brainstorm names for your new pet that will always remind them of what they've learned during this devotion. For example, you might name it "Lively," "Jailbird," "Grace," or "Thankful." Then give the pet a family hug as you pray, thanking God for saving your lives and allowing you to save your pet's life.

51.

Count Your Blessings

Focus: Reflecting on God's goodness

Scripture Reference: Psalm 111

   Here's a great way to reflect on God's blessings in your family and get a head start on your holiday mailings as well. This psalm and activity focus on recognizing the good things God does for his followers. Use this devotion to help your family concentrate on God's blessings in the past year and to share this good news with others.

Equipment: Paper, pens, and a Bible

Exploration: One or two days before this devotion let your family members know that you'll be preparing a family newsletter together. This will give everyone the opportunity to think about what they'd like to share in the newsletter. You may suggest to older family members that they begin writing their thoughts beforehand so they'll be ready to complete the newsletter during the devotion.

When you're ready to begin, pass out paper and pens and have each person write a column for a family newsletter. In addition to the normal updates on school, jobs, and the like, have family members tell what good things God has done this year in their lives. Tell everyone to include what they're learning about God, themselves, and others from these blessings. Children unable to write can dictate their thoughts to an older family member, or draw pictures of things God has done.

When everyone has finished, compile these columns by typing them onto one sheet of paper or cutting and pasting each person's handwritten words (or pictures) onto one page. Add a greeting, then photocopy and get them ready to send out to friends and relatives. (Addressing envelopes could also be part of this activity.)

Send out your family newsletter in late November or early December to kick off the holiday season and to recognize the greatest blessing God gave—himself.

Discovery: Sometime during your work, pause and read Psalm 111 together and discuss these questions:
- How many blessings does the writer see God giving?
- What do you think the psalmist learned about God from the good things God did?
- Why do you think God has done good things for us this past year, both as individuals and as a family?
- What can we learn about God and from the ways God has blessed us this year?

■ What can we learn about ourselves from the way we respond to God's blessings?

Prayer: Read aloud your finished newsletter, pausing after each person's column to let God know you appreciate the blessings he provides for your lives.

52.

Christmas Presence

Focus: The birth of Jesus

Scripture Reference: Luke 2:1-20

No event has affected humankind like the birth of this one baby. In a stable near an inn, the Creator of all became the created. The omnipotent God became a helpless infant. A candle of hope for all men, women, and children flickered and burst into flame. God had given himself as the first Christmas present ever.

It's easy to lose the significance of that simple event. Shopping lists, parties, feasts, and everyday worries cloud the story of God's love from our sight. Yet in the story itself remains the ageless, triumphant news—Joy to the world! The Lord has come! Use this devotion to reintroduce your family to the joy found in the story of a baby born in a manger.

Equipment: In addition to Bibles, gather the items listed below and wrap them as small gifts. Number each gift on the outside of its wrapping according to this list:

1. a pen
2. a ring (an inexpensive toy ring, or one borrowed from a family member)
3. strips of cloth (perhaps pieces of an old sheet or towel)
4. a flashlight

5. a Christmas songbook or recording of Christmas hymns (If neither of these is available, simply write the titles of your family's favorite Christmas songs on a piece of paper.)

Exploration: Have family members take turns opening the gifts in numerical order. After each gift is unwrapped, have the person opening it guess what the object has to do with the Christmas story. Then read the appropriate Scripture noted below to see if the symbol was correctly guessed.

■ Gift 1 (pen) represents writing names in the register (census). Read Luke 2:1-4.
■ Gift 2 (ring) represents the engagement of Joseph and Mary. Read Luke 2:5.
■ Gift 3 (cloth) represents the cloth in which Mary wrapped baby Jesus. Read Luke 2:6-7.
■ Gift 4 (flashlight) represents the glory of the Lord shining around the shepherds. Read Luke 2:8-12.
■ Gift 5 (songbook or recording) represents the songs of praise the angels sang and the praises of the shepherds. Read Luke 2:13-20.

Discovery: After you've finished telling the Christmas story, discuss these questions:
■ What do you think the place Jesus was born was like? How do you think Mary felt about having a baby there?
■ Imagine you were one of the shepherds that night. How would you have responded when angels suddenly appeared?
■ Read verse 19 again. Why were these events so important that Mary treasured them?
■ In what way is Jesus a "present" to you each day of the year?
■ How can you be a "present" to others?

Prayer: Take time out to prayerfully sing and thank God for his "Christmas Presence" each day of the year. Use the Christmas songbook or recording of Christmas hymns to help you. Close by asking God to help your family celebrate the present of Jesus each day of the year.

Index of Scripture References